The UK Ninja Dual Zone Air Fryer Cookbook 2023

The Complete Guide Of Everyday Homemade Air Fryer Meals With 1000 Days Easy & Healthy Air Fryer Recipes incl. Side Dishes, Desserts and More

Demi Sullivan

Copyright© 2023 By Demi Sullivan

All rights reserved worldwide.
No part of this book may be reproduced or transmitted in any form or by any means, electronic or mechanical, including photo- copying, recording or by any information storage and retrieval system, without written permission from the publisher, except for the inclusion of brief quotations in a review.

Warning-Disclaimer
The purpose of this book is to educate and entertain. The author or publisher does not guarantee that anyone following the techniques, suggestions, tips, ideas, or strategies will become successful. The author and publisher shall have neither liability or responsibility to anyone with respect to any loss or damage caused, or alleged to be caused, directly or indirectly by the information contained in this book.

Table of Contents

INTRODUCTION   1

Unleashing the Power of Your Ninja Dual Zone Air Fryer 1
Benefits of the Dual Independent Cooking Zones 2
Embarking on this Culinary Adventure 4

Chapter 1 Breakfasts   5

Egg White Cups 6
Breakfast Cobbler 6
Greek Bagels 6
Sausage and Egg Breakfast Burrito 7
All-in-One Toast & Denver Omelette 7
Parmesan Ranch Risotto 7
Cheddar-Ham-Corn Muffins 8
Apple Rolls 8
Red Pepper and Feta Frittata 8
Wholemeal Blueberry Muffins 8
Blueberry Cobbler 9
Pizza Eggs & Spinach Omelet 9
Portobello Eggs Benedict & Bacon Eggs on the Go 9
Super Easy Bacon Cups & Western Frittata 10
Cauliflower Avocado Toast & Breakfast Pitta 10
Strawberry Tarts 11
Bourbon Vanilla French Toast 11
Oat and Chia Porridge 11
Pancake Cake 11
Butternut Squash and Ricotta Frittata 12

Chapter 2 Family Favorites   13

Churro Bites 14
Veggie Tuna Melts 14
Berry Cheesecake 14
Cajun Shrimp 14
Beef Jerky 15
Avocado and Egg Burrito 15
Mixed Berry Crumble 15
Pork Burgers with Red Cabbage Salad 15
Scallops with Green Vegetables 15
Apple Pie Egg Rolls 16

Chapter 3 Fast and Easy Everyday Favourites   17

Traditional Queso Fundido 18
Cheesy Baked Grits 18
Beetroot Salad with Lemon Vinaigrette 18
Easy Devils on Horseback 18
Baked Chorizo Scotch Eggs 19
Air Fried Broccoli & Simple Pea Delight 19
Air Fried Shishito Peppers 19
Air Fried Tortilla Chips 19
Purple Potato Chips with Rosemary 20
Crunchy Fried Okra 20
Sweet Corn and Carrot Fritters 20
Herb-Roasted Veggies 20
Easy Roasted Asparagus 21
Scalloped Veggie Mix 21

Chapter 4 Poultry — 22

- Brazilian Tempero Baiano Chicken Drumsticks 23
- Korean Flavour Glazed Chicken Wings 23
- Chicken and Avocado Fajitas 23
- Turkey and Cranberry Quesadillas 24
- French Garlic Chicken 24
- Jerk Chicken Thighs 24
- Stuffed Turkey Roulade 24
- Chicken Wings with Piri Piri Sauce 25
- Indian Fennel Chicken 25
- Bruschetta Chicken 25
- Apricot-Glazed Turkey Tenderloin 25
- Chicken Parmesan 26
- Stuffed Chicken Florentine 26
- Honey-Glazed Chicken Thighs 26
- Sweet and Spicy Turkey Meatballs 26
- Greek Chicken Souvlaki 27
- Chicken Chimichangas 27
- Chicken Breasts with Asparagus, Beans, and Rocket ... 27
- Curried Orange Honey Chicken 28
- Coconut Chicken Wings with Mango Sauce 28
- Italian Crispy Chicken 28
- Tex-Mex Chicken Roll-Ups 29
- Korean Honey Wings 29
- Hawaiian Huli Huli Chicken 29
- Chicken Enchiladas 30

Chapter 5 Fish and Seafood — 31

- Seasoned Breaded Prawns 32
- Roasted Cod with Lemon-Garlic Potatoes 32
- Crab-Stuffed Avocado Boats 32
- Salmon with Fennel and Carrot 33
- Tortilla Prawn Tacos 33
- Parmesan-Crusted Halibut Fillets 33
- Pecan-Crusted Catfish 33
- Sole and Cauliflower Fritters 34
- Pesto Fish Pie 34
- Classic Prawns Empanadas 34
- Sole Fillets 34
- Crunchy Fish Sticks 35
- Calamari with Hot Sauce & Cornmeal-Crusted Trout Fingers 35
- Oregano Tilapia Fingers 35
- Prawns with Swiss Chard 35
- Blackened Fish 36
- Herbed Prawns Pita 36
- Prawn Kebabs 36
- Prawns with Smoky Tomato Dressing 36
- Cajun Catfish Cakes with Cheese 36
- Italian Tuna Roast 37
- Fish Gratin 37
- Lemony Salmon 37
- Golden Beer-Battered Cod 37

Chapter 6 Beef, Pork, and Lamb — 38

- Chinese-Style Baby Back Ribs 39
- Spicy Lamb Sirloin Chops 39
- Spicy Bavette Steak with Zhoug 39
- Spicy Rump Steak 40
- Fruited Ham 40
- Italian Sausages with Peppers and Onions 40
- Fillet with Crispy Shallots 40
- Spice-Rubbed Pork Loin 41
- Mozzarella Stuffed Beef and Pork Meatballs 41
- Sesame Beef Lettuce Tacos 41
- Peppercorn-Crusted Beef Fillet 41
- Kielbasa Sausage with Pineapple and Peppers 42
- Steak, Broccoli, and Mushroom Rice Bowls 42
- Steak with Bell Pepper 42
- Air Fryer Chicken-Fried Steak 42
- Bacon-Wrapped Hot Dogs with Mayo-Ketchup Sauce 43
- Lamb Burger with Feta and Olives 43
- Beef Burger 43
- Herb-Roasted Beef Tips with Onions 43
- Teriyaki Rump Steak with Broccoli and Capsicum 44
- Minute Steak Roll-Ups 44
- Fajita Meatball Lettuce Wraps 44
- Marinated Steak Tips with Mushrooms 44
- Vietnamese "Shaking" Beef 45
- Greek-Style Meatloaf 45

Chapter 7 Snacks and Appetizers — 46

- Browned Ricotta with Capers and Lemon 47
- Rumaki 47
- Crunchy Basil White Beans 47
- Sausage Balls with Cheese 47
- Pickle Chips 48
- Authentic Scotch Eggs 48
- Roasted Pearl Onion Dip 48
- Crispy Green Bean Fries with Lemon-Yoghurt Sauce 48
- Garlic-Roasted Tomatoes and Olives 49
- Prawns Egg Rolls 49
- Black Bean Corn Dip 49
- Stuffed Fried Mushrooms 49
- Spicy Tortilla Chips 50
- Crispy Green Tomatoes with Horseradish 50
- String Bean Fries 50
- Italian Rice Balls 50
- Cheese Drops 51
- Bacon-Wrapped Prawns and Jalapeño Chillies ... 51
- Dark Chocolate and Cranberry Granola Bars ... 51
- Mixed Vegetables Pot Stickers 51
- Fried Artichoke Hearts 52
- Prawns Toasts with Sesame Seeds 52
- Root Veggie Chips with Herb Salt & Grilled Ham and Cheese on Raisin Bread 52
- Prawns Pirogues 53

Chapter 8 Vegetables and Sides — 54

- Broccoli with Sesame Dressing 55
- Golden Pickles 55
- Chermoula-Roasted Beetroots 55
- Roasted Radishes with Sea Salt 55
- Parmesan-Rosemary Radishes 56
- Mashed Sweet Potato Tots 56
- Broccoli-Cheddar Twice-Baked Potatoes 56
- Rosemary New Potatoes 56
- Stuffed Red Peppers with Herbed Ricotta and Tomatoes 56
- Crispy Green Beans 57
- Burger Bun for One & Cheddar Broccoli with Bacon 57
- Cheesy Loaded Broccoli & Corn and Coriander Salad 57
- Bacon Potatoes and Green Beans 58
- Roasted Grape Tomatoes and Asparagus 58
- Asian Tofu Salad 58
- Parmesan Mushrooms 58
- Hawaiian Brown Rice 58
- Brussels Sprouts with Pecans and Gorgonzola ... 59
- Green Peas with Mint 59
- Glazed Sweet Potato Bites 59
- Crispy Courgette Sticks 59
- Dinner Rolls 59
- Courgette Balls 60

Chapter 9 Vegetarian Mains — 61

- Crispy Tofu 62
- Roasted Vegetables with Rice 62
- Caprese Aubergine Stacks 62
- Cayenne Tahini Kale 62
- Courgette and Spinach Croquettes 63
- Crispy Fried Okra with Chilli 63
- Buffalo Cauliflower Bites with Blue Cheese 63
- Parmesan Artichokes 63
- Whole Roasted Lemon Cauliflower 63
- Broccoli with Garlic Sauce 64
- Fried Root Vegetable Medley with Thyme 64
- Cheese Stuffed Courgette 64

Chapter 10 Desserts — 65

- Grilled Pineapple Dessert 66
- Baked Cheesecake 66
- Brownies for Two 66
- Butter Flax Cookies 66
- Apple Hand Pies 67
- Pumpkin Spice Pecans 67
- Mixed Berry Hand Pies 67
- Vanilla Scones 67
- Pumpkin Cookie with Cream Cheese Frosting ... 68
- Eggless Farina Cake 68
- Fried Cheesecake Bites 68
- Zucchini Bread 68
- Apple Fries 69
- Almond Shortbread 69
- Biscuit-Base Cheesecake 69

INTRODUCTION

Congratulations on your new Ninja Dual Zone Air Fryer! You've chosen a versatile and innovative kitchen appliance that will revolutionize the way you cook and enjoy your favorite foods. This cookbook is your ultimate guide to unlocking the full potential of your air fryer, allowing you to create delicious, crispy, and healthier meals with ease.

Unleashing the Power of Your Ninja Dual Zone Air Fryer

Prepare to unlock the incredible features and capabilities of your Ninja Dual Zone Air Fryer. Together, we will embark on a journey to understand the inner workings of this remarkable appliance and learn how to harness its power to create mouthwatering meals.

The Dual Zone cooking functionality is a game-changer. With two independent cooking zones at your disposal, you can simultaneously prepare two different dishes without any flavor transfer. It's like having two air fryers working in perfect harmony, providing you with unmatched flexibility and efficiency in the kitchen. Say goodbye to the hassle of waiting for one dish to finish before starting another – with your Ninja Dual Zone Air Fryer, multitasking becomes a breeze.

Let's not forget about the rapid hot air circulation, a signature feature of air frying. This advanced technology ensures that your food cooks evenly and achieves that coveted crispy, golden-brown texture. It's incredible how this appliance can deliver such delicious results with significantly less oil than traditional frying methods, making your meals healthier without compromising on taste.

Now, let's dive deeper into the temperature settings and cooking times. Understanding the nuances of these controls is crucial to achieving culinary perfection. With precise temperature control, you can customize the cooking conditions to suit the specific requirements of each dish. From delicate seafood to hearty meats, your Ninja Dual Zone Air Fryer empowers you to master a wide range of recipes with ease.

As we navigate the intricacies of your air fryer, we'll also explore the benefits of proper food placement and air flow management. Maximizing the efficiency of your cooking process is key to achieving optimal results. By strategically positioning your ingredients and ensuring adequate air circulation, you'll achieve consistent and mouthwatering outcomes every time you use your Ninja Dual Zone Air Fryer.

Maintenance is another essential aspect of owning this appliance. We'll cover tips and tricks to keep your air fryer in pristine condition, ensuring its longevity and continued performance. From cleaning the cooking baskets to caring for the heating elements, you'll learn how to maintain your Ninja Dual Zone Air Fryer and enjoy its benefits for years to come.

Together, we will unlock the full potential of your Ninja Dual Zone Air Fryer, empowering you to become a culinary master in your own kitchen. Get ready to unleash the power of this remarkable appliance and elevate your cooking game to new heights of flavor and convenience.

Benefits of the Dual Independent Cooking Zones

The dual independent cooking zones of your Ninja Dual Zone Air Fryer offer a multitude of benefits that elevate your cooking experience to new heights. These innovative zones provide you with the ability to cook two different dishes simultaneously without any flavor transfer. Let's explore the advantages of this unique feature:

♦ Enhanced Convenience: With the dual independent cooking zones, you can say goodbye to the time-consuming process of waiting for one dish to finish cooking before starting another. Whether you're preparing a main course and a side dish or catering to different dietary preferences in your household, the dual zones allow you to multitask and save valuable time in the kitchen. This means you can have a complete meal ready to serve all at once, minimizing the need for additional cooking steps or juggling multiple appliances.

♦ Efficient Meal Preparation: By utilizing the dual cooking zones, you can increase your cooking capacity and efficiency. The ability to cook two separate dishes at once not only saves time but also allows you to maximize the use of your air fryer's cooking space. This is especially useful when entertaining guests or when you have a larger quantity of food to prepare. You can effortlessly whip up a variety of dishes without the need for multiple rounds of cooking or using additional kitchen appliances.

♦ No Flavor Transfer: One of the most significant advantages of the dual independent cooking zones is the elimination of flavor transfer between dishes. Each zone operates independently, ensuring that the flavors and aromas of one dish do not infiltrate the other. This means you can confidently cook contrasting flavors or ingredients side by side without worrying about unwanted taste mingling. From sweet and savory combinations to accommodating different dietary restrictions, the dual zones provide you with the freedom to explore a wide range of flavors without compromise.

♦ Customized Cooking Conditions: The dual independent cooking zones allow you to customize the cooking conditions for each dish. You can set different temperatures and cooking times for each zone, ensuring that each item receives the optimal cooking environment it requires. This flexibility is particularly useful when preparing dishes with varying cooking requirements, such as delicate seafood alongside heartier meats or vegetables. You have complete control over the cooking process, allowing you to achieve perfect results for each dish.

The benefits of the dual independent cooking zones in your Ninja Dual Zone Air Fryer go beyond convenience and efficiency. They provide you with the freedom to create diverse and flavorful meals while maintaining distinct tastes and textures. Embrace the power of this feature and explore the endless possibilities it offers to elevate your culinary adventures in the kitchen.

Embarking on this Culinary Adventure

In this cookbook, you'll embark on a culinary journey with your Ninja Dual Zone Air Fryer, unlocking the full potential of its dual independent cooking zones. Discover the unparalleled convenience of cooking two dishes simultaneously without flavor transfer. Maximize efficiency, save time, and explore a wide range of flavors and textures. Customize cooking conditions to perfection, ensuring each dish is cooked to its unique requirements. With the power of the dual zones, you'll elevate your cooking game and create impressive meals that will delight your taste buds. Get ready to harness the power of the dual independent cooking zones and revolutionize your cooking experience.

Chapter 1 Breakfasts

Chapter 1 Breakfasts

Egg White Cups

Prep time: 10 minutes | Cook time: 15 minutes | Serves 4

475 ml 100% liquid egg whites
3 tablespoons salted butter, melted
¼ teaspoon salt
¼ teaspoon onion granules
½ medium plum tomato, cored and diced
120 g chopped fresh spinach leaves

1. In a large bowl, whisk egg whites with butter, salt, and onion granules. Stir in tomato and spinach, then pour evenly into four ramekins greased with cooking spray. 2. Place ramekins into one of the drawers of the fryer. Adjust the temperature to 150°C and bake for 15 minutes. Eggs will be fully cooked and firm in the center when done. Serve warm.

Breakfast Cobbler

Prep time: 20 minutes | Cook time: 30 minutes | Serves 4

Filling:

280 g sausage meat, crumbled
60 g minced onions
2 cloves garlic, minced
½ teaspoon fine sea salt
½ teaspoon ground black pepper
1 (230 g) package soft cheese (or soft cheese style spread for dairy-free), softened
180 g beef or chicken stock

Biscuits:

3 large egg whites
90 g blanched almond flour
1 teaspoon baking powder
¼ teaspoon fine sea salt
2½ tablespoons very cold unsalted butter, cut into ¼-inch pieces
Fresh thyme leaves, for garnish

1. Preheat the air fryer to 200°C. 2. Place the sausage, onions, and garlic in a pie pan. Using your hands, break up the sausage into small pieces and spread it evenly throughout the pie pan. Season with the salt and pepper. Place the pan in the air fryer and bake for 5 minutes. 3. While the sausage cooks, place the soft cheese and stock in a food processor or blender and purée until smooth. 4. Remove the pork from the air fryer and use a fork or metal spatula to crumble it more. Pour the soft cheese mixture into the sausage and stir to combine. Set aside. 5. Make the biscuits: Place the egg whites in a medium-sized mixing bowl or the bowl of a stand mixer and whip with a hand mixer or stand mixer until stiff peaks form. 6. In a separate medium-sized bowl, whisk together the almond flour, baking powder, and salt, then cut in the butter. When you are done, the mixture should still have chunks of butter. Gently fold the flour mixture into the egg whites with a rubber spatula. 7. Use a large spoon or ice cream scoop to scoop the dough into 4 equal-sized biscuits, making sure the butter is evenly distributed. Place the biscuits on top of the sausage and cook in the air fryer for 5 minutes, then turn the heat down to 160°C and bake for another 17 to 20 minutes, until the biscuits are golden brown. Serve garnished with fresh thyme leaves. 8. Store leftovers in an airtight container in the refrigerator for up to 3 days. Reheat in a preheated 180°C air fryer for 5 minutes, or until warmed through.

Greek Bagels

Prep time: 10 minutes | Cook time: 10 minutes | Makes 2 bagels

60 g self-raising flour, plus more for dusting
120 ml natural yoghurt
1 egg
1 tablespoon water
4 teaspoons sesame seeds or za'atar
Cooking oil spray
1 tablespoon butter, melted

1. In a large bowl, using a wooden spoon, stir together the flour and yoghurt until a tacky dough forms. Transfer the dough to a lightly floured work surface and roll the dough into a ball. 2. Cut the dough into 2 pieces and roll each piece into a log. Form each log into a bagel shape, pinching the ends together. 3. In a small bowl, whisk the egg and water. Brush the egg wash on the bagels. 4. Sprinkle 2 teaspoons of the toppings on each bagel and gently press it into the dough. 5. Insert the crisper plate into one of the baskets and the basket into the unit. Preheat the unit by selecting BAKE, setting the temperature to 170°C, and setting the time to 3 minutes. Select START/STOP to begin. 6. Once the unit is preheated, spray the crisper plate with cooking spray. Drizzle the bagels with the butter and place them into the basket. 7. Select BAKE, set the temperature to 170°C, and set the time to 10 minutes. Select START/STOP to begin. 8. When the cooking is complete, the bagels should be lightly golden on the outside. Serve warm.

Sausage and Egg Breakfast Burrito

Prep time: 5 minutes | Cook time: 30 minutes | Serves 6

6 eggs
Salt and pepper, to taste
Cooking oil
120 g chopped red pepper
120 g chopped green pepper
230 g chicken sausage meat (removed from casings)
120 ml tomato salsa
6 medium (8-inch) wheat tortillas
120 g grated Cheddar cheese

1. In a medium bowl, whisk the eggs. Add salt and pepper to taste. 2. Place a skillet on medium-high heat. Spray with cooking oil. Add the eggs. Scramble for 2 to 3 minutes, until the eggs are fluffy. Remove the eggs from the skillet and set aside. 3. If needed, spray the skillet with more oil. Add the chopped red and green bell peppers. Cook for 2 to 3 minutes, until the peppers are soft. 4. Add the sausage meat to the skillet. Break the sausage into smaller pieces using a spatula or spoon. Cook for 3 to 4 minutes, until the sausage is brown. 5. Add the tomato salsa and scrambled eggs. Stir to combine. Remove the skillet from heat. 6. Spoon the mixture evenly onto the tortillas. 7. To form the burritos, fold the sides of each tortilla in toward the middle and then roll up from the bottom. You can secure each burrito with a toothpick. Or you can moisten the outside edge of the tortilla with a small amount of water. I prefer to use a cooking brush, but you can also dab with your fingers. 8. Spray the burritos with cooking oil and place them half in zone 1, the remaining in zone 2. In zone 1, select Air fry button, adjust temperature to 200ºC, set time to 8 minutes. In zone 2, select Match Cook and press Start. Do not stack. Cook the burritos in batches if they do not all fit in the basket. 9. Open the air fryer and flip the burritos. Cook for an additional 2 minutes or until crisp. 10. If necessary, repeat steps 8 and 9 for the remaining burritos. 11. Sprinkle the Cheddar cheese over the burritos. Cool before serving.

All-in-One Toast & Denver Omelette

Prep time: 15 minutes | Cook time: 10 minutes

All-in-one Toast | Serves 1:

1 strip bacon, diced
1 slice 1-inch thick bread
1 egg
Salt and freshly ground black pepper, to taste
60 g grated Monterey Jack or Chedday cheese

Denver Omelette | Serves 1:

2 large eggs
60 ml unsweetened, unflavoured almond milk
¼ teaspoon fine sea salt
⅛ teaspoon ground black pepper
60 g diced gammon (omit for vegetarian)
60 g diced green and red peppers
2 tablespoons diced spring onions, plus more for garnish
60 g grated Cheddar cheese (about 30 g) (omit for dairy-free)
Quartered cherry tomatoes, for serving (optional)

Prepare for All-in-one Toast:

1. Preheat the air fryer to 200ºC on zone 1 drawer.
2. Air fry the bacon for 3 minutes, shaking zone 1 drawer once or twice while it cooks. Remove the bacon to a paper towel-lined plate and set it aside.
3. Use a sharp paring knife to score a large circle in the middle of the slice of bread, cutting halfway through, but not all the way through to the cutting board. Press down on the circle in the center of the bread slice to create an indentation.
4. Transfer the slice of bread, hole side up, to zone 1 drawer. Crack the egg into the center of the bread, and season with salt and pepper.

Prepare for Denver Omelette:

1. Preheat the air fryer to 180ºC on zone 2 drawer.
2. Grease a cake pan and set aside. In a small bowl, use a fork to whisk together the eggs, almond milk, salt, and pepper. Add the ham, peppers, and spring onions. Pour the mixture into the greased pan. Add the cheese on top (if using).
3. Place the pan in zone 2 drawer.

Cook:

1. In zone 1, adjust the air fryer temperature to 190ºC and air fry for 5 minutes.
2. In zone 2, adjust the air fryer temperature to 180ºC and air fry for 8 minutes.
3. Press SYNC, then press Start.
4. Sprinkle grated cheese around the edges of the All-in-One Toast in zone 1, and top with cooked bacon. Air fry for 1-2 more minutes to melt the cheese and finish cooking the egg.
5. Remove the Denver Omelette from the pan and place it on a serving plate. Garnish with spring onions and serve with cherry tomatoes if desired.

Parmesan Ranch Risotto

Prep time: 10 minutes | Cook time: 30 minutes | Serves 2

1 tablespoon rapeseed oil
1 clove garlic, minced
1 tablespoon unsalted butter
1 onion, diced
180 g Arborio rice
475 g chicken stock, boiling
120 g Parmesan cheese, grated

1. Preheat the air fryer to 200ºC. 2. Grease a round baking tin with rapeseed oil and stir in the garlic, butter, and onion. 3. Transfer the tin to zone 1 drawer and bake for 4 minutes. Add the rice and bake for 4 more minutes. 4. Turn the air fryer to 160ºC and pour in the chicken stock. Cover and bake for 22 minutes. 5. Scatter with cheese and serve.

Cheddar-Ham-Corn Muffins

Prep time: 10 minutes | Cook time: 6 to 8 minutes per batch | Makes 8 muffins

- 90 g cornmeal/polenta
- 30 g flour
- 1½ teaspoons baking powder
- ¼ teaspoon salt
- 1 egg, beaten
- 2 tablespoons rapeseed oil
- 120 ml milk
- 120 g grated mature Cheddar cheese
- 120 g diced gammon
- 8 foil muffin cups, liners removed and sprayed with cooking spray

1. Preheat the air fryer to 200ºC. 2. In a medium bowl, stir together the cornmeal, flour, baking powder, and salt. 3. Add egg, oil, and milk to dry ingredients and mix well. 4. Stir in grated cheese and diced gammon. 5. Divide batter among the muffin cups. 6. Place 4 filled muffin cups in zone 1 drawer and bake for 5 minutes. 7. Reduce temperature to 170ºC and bake for 1 to 2 minutes or until toothpick inserted in center of muffin comes out clean. 8. Repeat steps 6 and 7 to cook remaining muffins.

Apple Rolls

Prep time: 20 minutes | Cook time: 20 to 24 minutes | Makes 12 rolls

Apple Rolls:

- 235 g plain flour, plus more for dusting
- 2 tablespoons granulated sugar
- 1 teaspoon salt
- 3 tablespoons butter, at room temperature
- 180 ml milk, whole or semi-skimmed
- 95 g packed light soft brown sugar
- 1 teaspoon ground cinnamon
- 1 large Granny Smith apple, peeled and diced
- 1 to 2 tablespoons oil

Icing:

- 75 g icing sugar
- ½ teaspoon vanilla extract
- 2 to 3 tablespoons milk, whole or semi-skimmed

Make the Apple Rolls 1. In a large bowl, whisk the flour, granulated sugar, and salt until blended. Stir in the butter and milk briefly until a sticky dough forms. 2. In a small bowl, stir together the soft brown sugar, cinnamon, and apple. 3. Place a piece of parchment paper on a work surface and dust it with flour. Roll the dough on the prepared surface to ¼ inch thickness. 4. Spread the apple mixture over the dough. Roll up the dough jelly roll-style, pinching the ends to seal. Cut the dough into 12 rolls. 5. Preheat the air fryer to 160ºC. 6. Line the air fryer basket with parchment paper and spritz it with oil. Place rolls half in zone 1, the remaining in zone 2. In zone 1, select Air fry button. In zone 2, select Match Cook and press Start. 7. Bake for 5 minutes. Flip the rolls and bake for 5 to 7 minutes more until lightly browned. Repeat with the remaining rolls. Make the Icing 8. In a medium bowl, whisk the icing sugar, vanilla, and milk until blended. 9. Drizzle over the warm rolls.

Red Pepper and Feta Frittata

Prep time: 10 minutes | Cook time: 20 minutes | Serves 4

- rapeseed oil cooking spray
- 8 large eggs
- 1 medium red pepper, diced
- ½ teaspoon salt
- ½ teaspoon black pepper
- 1 garlic clove, minced
- 120 g feta, divided

1. Preheat the air fryer to 180ºC. Lightly coat the inside of a 6-inch round cake pan with rapeseed oil cooking spray. 2. In a large bowl, beat the eggs for 1 to 2 minutes, or until well combined. 3. Add the red pepper, salt, black pepper, and garlic to the eggs, and mix together until the red pepper is distributed throughout. 4. Fold in 60 ml the feta cheese. 5. Pour the egg mixture into the prepared cake pan, and sprinkle the remaining 60 ml feta over the top. 6. Place into zone 1 drawer and bake for 18 to 20 minutes, or until the eggs are set in the center. 7. Remove from the air fryer and allow to cool for 5 minutes before serving.

Wholemeal Blueberry Muffins

Prep time: 10 minutes | Cook time: 15 minutes | Serves 6

- rapeseed oil cooking spray
- 120 ml unsweetened applesauce
- 60 ml honey
- 120 ml non-fat natural yoghurt
- 1 teaspoon vanilla extract
- 1 large egg
- 350 g plus 1 tablespoon wholemeal, divided
- ½ teaspoon baking soda
- ½ teaspoon baking powder
- ½ teaspoon salt
- 120 g blueberries, fresh or frozen

1. Preheat the air fryer to 180ºC. Lightly coat the inside of six silicone muffin cups or a six-cup muffin tin with rapeseed oil cooking spray. 2. In a large bowl, combine the applesauce, honey, yoghurt, vanilla, and egg and mix until smooth. 3. Sift in 350 ml of the flour, the baking soda, baking powder, and salt into the wet mixture, then stir until just combined. 4. In a small bowl, toss the blueberries with the remaining 1 tablespoon flour, then fold the mixture into the muffin batter. 5. Divide the mixture evenly among the prepared muffin cups, and them place half in zone 1, the remaining in zone 2. In zone 1, select Air fry button, set time to 12 minutes to 15 minutes, or until golden brown on top and a toothpick inserted into the middle of one of the muffins comes out clean. In zone 2, select Match Cook and press Start. 6. Allow to cool for 5 minutes before serving.

Blueberry Cobbler

Prep time: 5 minutes | Cook time: 15 minutes | Serves 4

40 g wholemeal pastry flour
¾ teaspoon baking powder
Dash sea salt
120 ml semi-skimmed milk
2 tablespoons pure maple syrup
½ teaspoon vanilla extract
Cooking oil spray
120 g fresh blueberries
60 g granola

1. In a medium bowl, whisk the flour, baking powder, and salt. Add the milk, maple syrup, and vanilla and gently whisk, just until thoroughly combined. 2. Preheat the unit by selecting BAKE, setting the temperature to 180°C, and setting the time to 3 minutes. Select START/STOP to begin. 3. Spray a 6-by-2-inch round baking pan with cooking oil and pour the batter into the pan. Top evenly with the blueberries and granola. 4. Once the unit is preheated, place the pan into the basket. 5. Select BAKE, set the temperature to 180°C, and set the time to 15 minutes. Select START/STOP to begin. 6. When the cooking is complete, the cobbler should be nicely browned and a knife inserted into the middle should come out clean. Enjoy plain or topped with a little vanilla yoghurt.

Pizza Eggs & Spinach Omelet

Prep time: 10 minutes | Cook time: 12 minutes

Pizza Eggs | Serves 2:

235 g grated Cheddar cheese
7 slices pepperoni, chopped
1 large egg, whisked
¼ teaspoon dried oregano
¼ teaspoon dried parsley
¼ teaspoon garlic powder
¼ teaspoon salt

Spinach Omelet | Serves 2:

4 large eggs
350 g chopped fresh spinach leaves
2 tablespoons peeled and chopped brown onion
2 tablespoons salted butter, melted
120 g grated mild Cheddar cheese
¼ teaspoon salt

Prepare for Pizza Eggs:

1. Place Mozzarella in a single layer on the bottom of an ungreased round nonstick baking dish. Scatter pepperoni over cheese, then pour egg evenly around baking dish.
2. Sprinkle with remaining ingredients and place into zone 1 drawer.

Prepare for Spinach Omelet:

1. In an ungreased round nonstick baking dish, whisk eggs. Stir in spinach, onion, butter, Cheddar, and salt.
2. Place dish into zone 2 drawer.

Cook:

1. In zone 1, set the temperature to 170°C, set the time to 10 minutes.
2. In zone 2, set the temperature to 160°C, set the time to 12 minutes.
3. Press SYNC, then press Start.
4. The dish will be done when the cheese is brown and the egg is set.
Let it cool in the dish for 5 minutes before serving.
5. The omelet will be done when it is browned on the top and firm in the middle. Slice the omelet in half and serve warm on two medium plates.

Portobello Eggs Benedict & Bacon Eggs on the Go

Prep time: 15 minutes | Cook time: 15 minutes

Portobello Eggs Benedict | Serves 2:

1 tablespoon rapeseed oil
2 cloves garlic, minced
¼ teaspoon dried thyme
2 portobello mushrooms, stems removed and gills scraped out
2 vine tomatoes, halved lengthwise
Salt and freshly ground black pepper, to taste
2 large eggs
2 tablespoons grated Pecorino Romano cheese
1 tablespoon chopped fresh parsley, for garnish
1 teaspoon truffle oil (optional)

Bacon Eggs on the Go | Serves 1:

2 eggs
110 g bacon, cooked
Salt and ground black pepper, to taste

Prepare for Portobello Eggs Benedict:

1. Preheat the air fryer to 200°C on zone 1 drawer.
2. In a small bowl, combine the rapeseed oil, minced garlic, and dried thyme.
3. Brush the mixture over the portobello mushrooms and vine tomatoes until thoroughly coated.
4. Season with salt and freshly ground black pepper.
5. Arrange the vegetables, cut side up, in zone 1 drawer.

Prepare for Bacon Eggs on the Go:

1. Preheat the air fryer to 200°C on zone 2 drawer.
2. Place liners in a regular cupcake tin.
3. Crack an egg into each cup and add the cooked bacon.
4. Season with salt and ground black pepper.

Cook:

1. In zone 1, set the temperature to 200°C, set the time to 10 to 14 minutes, or until the vegetables are tender and the whites of the eggs are firm.
2. In zone 2, set the temperature to 200°C, set the time to 15 minutes or until the eggs are set.
3. Serve the Portobello Eggs Benedict garnished with chopped fresh parsley and drizzled with truffle oil, if desired.

Super Easy Bacon Cups & Western Frittata

Prep time: 15 minutes | Cook time: 20 minutes

Super Easy Bacon Cup | Serves 2:

3 slices bacon, cooked, sliced in half
2 slices ham
1 slice tomato
2 eggs
2 teaspoons grated Parmesan cheese
Salt and ground black pepper, to taste

Western Frittata | Serves 1 to 2:

½ red or green pepper, cut into ½-inch chunks
1 teaspoon rapeseed oil
3 eggs, beaten
60 g grated Cheddar cheese
60 g diced cooked ham
Salt and freshly ground black pepper, to taste
1 teaspoon butter
1 teaspoon chopped fresh parsley

Prepare for Super Easy Bacon Cup:

1. Preheat the air fryer to 190ºC on zone 1 drawer
2. Line 2 greased muffin tins with 3 half-strips of bacon.
3. Place one slice of ham and half a slice of tomato in each muffin tin on top of the bacon.
4. Crack one egg on top of the tomato in each muffin tin.
5. Sprinkle each cup with half a teaspoon of grated Parmesan cheese. Sprinkle with salt and ground black pepper, if desired.

Prepare for Western Frittata:

1. Preheat the air fryer to 200ºC on zone 2 drawer.
2. Toss the pepper chunks with rapeseed oil and air fry for 6 minutes, shaking the basket once or twice during cooking to redistribute the ingredients.
3. While the peppers are cooking, beat the eggs well in a bowl.
4. Stir in the grated Cheddar cheese, diced ham, and season with salt and freshly ground black pepper.
5. Add the air-fried peppers to the egg mixture when they are done cooking.
6. Grease a cake pan with the butter and place it into zone 2 drawer using an aluminum sling to lower it.

Cook:

1. In zone 1, set the temperature to 190ºC, set the time to 20 minutes.
2. In zone 2, set the temperature to 190ºC, set the time to 12 minutes.
3. Press SYNC, then press Start.
4. Let the frittata sit in the air fryer for 5 minutes to cool and set up. Remove the cake pan from the air fryer and sprinkle with chopped fresh parsley. Serve immediately.
5. Remove the bacon cups from the air fryer and let them cool. Serve warm.

Cauliflower Avocado Toast & Breakfast Pitta

Prep time: 20 minutes | Cook time: 8 minutes

Cauliflower Avocado Toast | Serves 2

1 (40 g) steamer bag cauliflower
1 large egg
120 g grated Cheddar cheese
1 ripe medium avocado
½ teaspoon garlic powder
¼ teaspoon ground black pepper

Breakfast Pitta | Serves 2

1 wholemeal pitta
2 teaspoons rapeseed oil
½ shallot, diced
¼ teaspoon garlic, minced
1 large egg
¼ teaspoon dried oregano
¼ teaspoon dried thyme
⅛ teaspoon salt
2 tablespoons grated Parmesan cheese

Prepare for Cauliflower Avocado Toast:

1. Cook the cauliflower according to the package instructions. Remove from the bag and place it in cheesecloth or a clean towel to remove excess moisture.
2. Place the cauliflower in a large bowl and mix in the egg and grated Cheddar cheese.
3. Cut a piece of parchment paper to fit your air fryer basket. Separate the cauliflower mixture into two and place each portion on the parchment paper in two mounds. Press out the cauliflower mounds into a ¼-inch-thick rectangle.
4. Place the parchment paper in the zone 1 drawer.

Prepare for Breakfast Pitta:

1. Preheat the air fryer to 190ºC on zone 2 drawer.
2. Brush the top of the pitta with rapeseed oil, then spread the diced shallot and minced garlic over the pitta.
3. Crack the egg into a small bowl or ramekin and season it with dried oregano, dried thyme, and salt.
4. Place the pitta in the zone 2 drawer.

Cook:

1. In zone 1, set the temperature to 200ºC, set the time to 8 minutes.
2. In zone 2, set the temperature to 190ºC, set the time to 6 minutes.
3. Press SYNC, then press Start.
4. Flip the cauliflower halfway through the cooking time. When the timer beeps, remove the parchment paper and allow the cauliflower to cool for 5 minutes. Cut open the avocado, remove the pit, and scoop out the flesh into a medium bowl. Mash the avocado with garlic powder and ground black pepper.
Spread the mashed avocado onto the cauliflower rectangles. Serve immediately.
5. Allow the pitta to cool for 5 minutes before cutting it into pieces for serving.

Strawberry Tarts

Prep time: 15 minutes | Cook time: 10 minutes | Serves 6

2 refrigerated piecrusts	30 g soft cheese, at room temperature
120 g strawberry preserves	
1 teaspoon cornflour	3 tablespoons icing sugar
Cooking oil spray	Rainbow sprinkles, for decorating
120 ml low-fat vanilla yoghurt	

1. Place the piecrusts on a flat surface. Using a knife or pizza cutter, cut each piecrust into 3 rectangles, for 6 total. Discard any unused dough from the piecrust edges. 2. In a small bowl, stir together the preserves and cornflour. Mix well, ensuring there are no lumps of cornflour remaining. 3. Scoop 1 tablespoon of the strawberry mixture onto the top half of each piece of piecrust. 4. Fold the bottom of each piece up to enclose the filling. Using the back of a fork, press along the edges of each tart to seal. 5. Insert the crisper plate into the basket and the basket into the unit. Preheat the unit by selecting BAKE, setting the temperature to 190ºC, and setting the time to 3 minutes. Select START/STOP to begin. 6. Once the unit is preheated, spray the crisper plate with cooking oil. Pour the tarts half in zone 1, the remaining in zone 2. In zone 1, select Air fry button, adjust temperature to 190ºC, set time to 10 minutes. In zone 2, select Match Cook and press Start. Do not stack the tarts. 7. When the cooking is complete, the tarts should be light golden brown. Let the breakfast tarts cool fully before removing them from the basket. 8. Repeat steps 5, 6, and 7 for the remaining breakfast tarts. 9. In a small bowl, stir together the yoghurt, soft cheese, and icing sugar. Spread the breakfast tarts with the frosting and top with sprinkles.

Bourbon Vanilla French Toast

Prep time: 15 minutes | Cook time: 6 minutes | Serves 4

2 large eggs	2 tablespoons bourbon
2 tablespoons water	1 teaspoon vanilla extract
160 ml whole or semi-skimmed milk	8 (1-inch-thick) French bread slices
1 tablespoon butter, melted	Cooking spray

1. Preheat the air fryer to 160ºC. Line the air fryer basket with parchment paper and spray it with cooking spray. 2. Beat the eggs with the water in a shallow bowl until combined. Add the milk, melted butter, bourbon, and vanilla and stir to mix well. 3. Dredge 4 slices of bread in the batter, turning to coat both sides evenly. Transfer the bread slices onto the parchment paper. 4. Bake for 6 minutes until nicely browned. Flip the slices halfway through the cooking time. 5. Remove from the basket to a plate and repeat with the remaining 4 slices of bread. 6. Serve warm.

Oat and Chia Porridge

Prep time: 10 minutes | Cook time: 5 minutes | Serves 4

2 tablespoons peanut butter	1 L milk
4 tablespoons honey	475 g oats
1 tablespoon butter, melted	235 g chia seeds

1. Preheat the air fryer to 200ºC. 2. Put the peanut butter, honey, butter, and milk in a bowl and stir to mix. Add the oats and chia seeds and stir. 3. Transfer the mixture to a bowl and bake in one of the drawers of the fryer for 5 minutes. Give another stir before serving.

Pancake Cake

Prep time: 10 minutes | Cook time: 7 minutes | Serves 4

60 g blanched finely ground almond flour	softened
30 g powdered erythritol	1 large egg
½ teaspoon baking powder	½ teaspoon unflavoured gelatin
2 tablespoons unsalted butter,	½ teaspoon vanilla extract
	½ teaspoon ground cinnamon

1. In a large bowl, mix almond flour, erythritol, and baking powder. Add butter, egg, gelatin, vanilla, and cinnamon. Pour into a round baking pan. 2. Place pan into the air fryer basket. 3. Adjust the temperature to 150ºC and set the timer for 7 minutes. 4. When the cake is completely cooked, a toothpick will come out clean. Cut cake into four and serve.

Butternut Squash and Ricotta Frittata

Prep time: 10 minutes | Cook time: 33 minutes | Serves 2 to 3

235 ml cubed (½-inch) butternut squash (160 g)
2 tablespoons rapeseed oil
Coarse or flaky salt and freshly ground black pepper, to taste
4 fresh sage leaves, thinly sliced
6 large eggs, lightly beaten
120 g ricotta cheese
Cayenne pepper

1. In a bowl, toss the squash with the rapeseed oil and season with salt and black pepper until evenly coated. Sprinkle the sage on the bottom of a cake pan and place the squash on top. Place the pan in zone 1 drawer and bake at 200°C for 10 minutes. Stir to incorporate the sage, then cook until the squash is tender and lightly caramelized at the edges, about 3 minutes more. 2. Pour the eggs over the squash, dollop the ricotta all over, and sprinkle with cayenne. Bake at 150°C until the eggs are set and the frittata is golden brown on top, about 20 minutes. Remove the pan from the air fryer and cut the frittata into wedges to serve.

Chapter 2 Family Favorites

Chapter 2 Family Favorites

Churro Bites

Prep time: 5 minutes | Cook time: 6 minutes | Makes 36 bites

Oil, for spraying
1 (500 g) package frozen puffed pastry, thawed
180 g caster sugar
1 tablespoon ground cinnamon
90 g icing sugar
1 tablespoon milk

1. Preheat the air fryer to 200ºC. 2. Line the air fryer basket with parchment and spray lightly with oil. 3. Unfold the puff pastry onto a clean work surface. Using a sharp knife, cut the dough into 36 bite-size pieces. 4. Place the dough pieces in one layer half in zone 1, the remaining in zone 2 in the prepared basket, taking care not to let the pieces touch or overlap. 5. Cook for 3 minutes, flip, and cook for another 3 minutes, or until puffed and golden. In a small bowl, mix together the caster sugar and cinnamon. 6. In another small bowl, whisk together the icing sugar and milk. 7. Dredge the bites in the cinnamon-sugar mixture until evenly coated. 8. Serve with the icing on the side for dipping.

Veggie Tuna Melts

Prep time: 15 minutes | Cook time: 7 to 11 minutes | Serves 4

2 low-salt wholemeal English muffins, split
1 (170 g) can chunk light low-salt tuna, drained
235 g shredded carrot
80 g chopped mushrooms
2 spring onions, white and green parts, sliced
80 ml fat-free Greek yoghurt
2 tablespoons low-salt wholegrain mustard
2 slices low-salt low-fat Swiss cheese, halved

1. Place the English muffin halves in one of the air fryer baskets. 2. Air fry at 170ºC for 3 to 4 minutes, or until crisp. Remove from the basket and set aside. 3. In a medium bowl, thoroughly mix the tuna, carrot, mushrooms, spring onions, yoghurt, and mustard. 4. Top each half of the muffins with one-fourth of the tuna mixture and a half slice of Swiss cheese. 5. Air fry for 4 to 7 minutes, or until the tuna mixture is hot and the cheese melts and starts to brown. 6. Serve immediately.

Berry Cheesecake

Prep time: 5 minutes | Cook time: 10 minutes | Serves 4

Oil, for spraying
227 g soft white cheese
6 tablespoons sugar
1 tablespoon sour cream
1 large egg
½ teaspoon vanilla extract
¼ teaspoon lemon juice
120 g fresh mixed berries

1. Preheat the air fryer to 180ºC. 2. Line the air fryer basket with parchment and spray lightly with oil. 3. In a blender, combine the soft white cheese, sugar, sour cream, egg, vanilla, and lemon juice and blend until smooth. 4. Pour the mixture into a 4-inch springform pan. 5. Place the pan in the prepared basket. Cook for 8 to 10 minutes, or until only the very centre jiggles slightly when the pan is moved. 6. Refrigerate the cheesecake in the pan for at least 2 hours. 7. Release the sides from the springform pan, top the cheesecake with the mixed berries, and serve.

Cajun Shrimp

Prep time: 15 minutes | Cook time: 9 minutes | Serves 4

Oil, for spraying
450 g king prawns, peeled and deveined
1 tablespoon Cajun seasoning
170 g Polish sausage, cut into thick slices
½ medium courgette, cut into ¼-inch-thick slices
½ medium yellow squash or butternut squash, cut into ¼-inch-thick slices
1 green pepper, seeded and cut into 1-inch pieces
2 tablespoons olive oil
½ teaspoon salt

1. Preheat the air fryer to 200ºC. 2. Line the air fryer basket with parchment and spray lightly with oil. In a large bowl, toss together the shrimp and Cajun seasoning. 3. Add the kielbasa, courgette, squash, pepper, olive oil, and salt and mix well. 4. Transfer the mixture to the prepared basket, taking care not to overcrowd. 5. You may need to work in batches, depending on the size of your air fryer. 6. Cook for 9 minutes, shaking and stirring every 3 minutes. 7. Serve immediately.

Beef Jerky

Prep time: 30 minutes | Cook time: 2 hours | Serves 8

Oil, for spraying
450 g silverside, cut into thin, short slices
60 ml soy sauce
3 tablespoons packed light muscovado sugar
1 tablespoon minced garlic
1 teaspoon ground ginger
1 tablespoon water

1. Line the air fryer basket with parchment and spray lightly with oil. 2. Place the steak, soy sauce, brown sugar, garlic, ginger, and water in a zip-top plastic bag, seal, and shake well until evenly coated. 3. Refrigerate for 30 minutes. Place the steak in the prepared basket in a single layer. 4. You may need to work in batches, depending on the size of your air fryer. 5. Air fry at 80ºC for at least 2 hours. 6. Add more time if you like your jerky a bit tougher.

Avocado and Egg Burrito

Prep time: 10 minutes | Cook time: 3 to 5 minutes | Serves 4

2 hard-boiled egg whites, chopped
1 hard-boiled egg, chopped
1 avocado, peeled, pitted, and chopped
1 red pepper, chopped
3 tablespoons low-salt salsa, plus additional for serving (optional)
1 (34 g) slice low-salt, low-fat processed cheese, torn into pieces
4 low-salt wholemeal flour wraps

1. In a medium bowl, thoroughly mix the egg whites, egg, avocado, red pepper, salsa, and cheese. 2. Place the tortillas on a work surface and evenly divide the filling among them. 3. Fold in the edges and roll up. Secure the burritos with toothpicks if necessary. 4. Put the burritos in zone 1 drawer. 5. Air fry at 200ºC for 3 to 5 minutes, or until the burritos are light golden brown and crisp. 6. Serve with more salsa (if using).

Mixed Berry Crumble

Prep time: 10 minutes | Cook time: 11 to 16 minutes | Serves 4

120 g chopped fresh strawberries
120 g fresh blueberries
80 g frozen raspberries
1 tablespoon freshly squeezed lemon juice
1 tablespoon honey
80 g wholemeal plain flour
3 tablespoons light muscovado sugar
2 tablespoons unsalted butter, melted

1. In a baking pan, combine the strawberries, blueberries, and raspberries. 2. Drizzle with the lemon juice and honey. 3. In a small bowl, mix the pastry flour and brown sugar. 4. Stir in the butter and mix until crumbly. 5. Sprinkle this mixture over the fruit. 6. Bake at 190ºC for 11 to 16 minutes, or until the fruit is tender and bubbly and the topping is golden brown. 7. Serve warm.

Pork Burgers with Red Cabbage Salad

Prep time: 20 minutes | Cook time: 7 to 9 minutes | Serves 4

120 ml Greek yoghurt
2 tablespoons low-salt mustard, divided
1 tablespoon lemon juice
60 g sliced red cabbage
60 g grated carrots
450 g lean finely chopped pork
½ teaspoon paprika
235 g mixed salad leaves
2 small tomatoes, sliced
8 small low-salt wholemeal sandwich buns, cut in half

1. In a small bowl, combine the yoghurt, 1 tablespoon mustard, lemon juice, cabbage, and carrots; mix and refrigerate. 2. In a medium bowl, combine the pork, remaining 1 tablespoon mustard, and paprika. Form into 8 small patties. Put the sliders into one of the air fryer baskets. 3. Air fry at 200ºC for 7 to 9 minutes, or until the sliders register 74ºC as tested with a meat thermometer. 4. Assemble the burgers by placing some of the lettuce greens on a bun bottom. 5. Top with a tomato slice, the burgers, and the cabbage mixture. 6. Add the bun top and serve immediately.

Scallops with Green Vegetables

Prep time: 15 minutes | Cook time: 8 to 11 minutes | Serves 4

235 g green beans
235 g garden peas
235 g frozen chopped broccoli
2 teaspoons olive oil
½ teaspoon dried basil
½ teaspoon dried oregano
340 g sea scallops

1. In a large bowl, toss the green beans, peas, and broccoli with the olive oil. 2. Place in one of the air fryer baskets. 3. Air fry at 200ºC for 4 to 6 minutes, or until the vegetables are crisp-tender. 4. Remove the vegetables from the air fryer basket and sprinkle with the herbs. Set aside. 5. In the air fryer basket, put the scallops and air fry for 4 to 5 minutes, or until the scallops are firm and reach an internal temperature of just 64ºC on a meat thermometer. 6. Toss scallops with the vegetables and serve immediately.

Apple Pie Egg Rolls

Prep time: 10 minutes | Cook time: 8 minutes | Makes 6 rolls

Oil, for spraying
1 (600 g) can apple pie filling
1 tablespoon plain flour
½ teaspoon lemon juice
¼ teaspoon ground nutmeg
¼ teaspoon ground cinnamon
6 egg roll wrappers

1. Preheat the air fryer to 200ºC. 2.Line the air fryer basket with parchment and spray lightly with oil. 3.In a medium bowl, mix together the pie filling, flour, lemon juice, nutmeg, and cinnamon. 4.Lay out the egg roll wrappers on a work surface and spoon a dollop of pie filling in the centre of each. 5.Fill a small bowl with water. Dip your finger in the water and, working one at a time, moisten the edges of the wrappers. 6.Fold the wrapper like an envelope: First fold one corner into the centre. 7.Fold each side corner in, and then fold over the remaining corner, making sure each corner overlaps a bit and the moistened edges stay closed. 8.Use additional water and your fingers to seal any open edges. 9.Place the rolls half in zone 1, the remaining in zone 2, and spray liberally with oil. 10.You may need to work in batches, depending on the size of your air fryer. 11.Cook for 4 minutes, flip, spray with oil, and cook for another 4 minutes, or until crispy and golden brown. 12.Serve immediately.

Chapter 3 Fast and Easy Everyday Favourites

Traditional Queso Fundido

Prep time: 10 minutes | Cook time: 25 minutes | Serves 4

110 g fresh Mexican (or Spanish if unavailable) chorizo, casings removed
1 medium onion, chopped
3 cloves garlic, minced
235 g chopped tomato
2 jalapeños, deseeded and diced
2 teaspoons ground cumin
475 g shredded Oaxaca or Mozzarella cheese
120 ml half-and-half (60 g whole milk and 60 ml cream combined)
Celery sticks or tortilla chips, for serving

1. Preheat the air fryer to 200ºC. 2. In a baking tray, combine the chorizo, onion, garlic, tomato, jalapeños, and cumin. Stir to combine. 3. Place the pan in one of the air fryer baskets. 4. Air fry for 15 minutes, or until the sausage is cooked, stirring halfway through the cooking time to break up the sausage. 5. Add the cheese and half-and-half; stir to combine. 6. Air fry for 10 minutes, or until the cheese has melted. 7. Serve with celery sticks or tortilla chips.

Cheesy Baked Grits

Prep time: 10 minutes | Cook time: 12 minutes | Serves 6

180 ml hot water
2 (28 g) packages instant grits
1 large egg, beaten
1 tablespoon melted butter
2 cloves garlic, minced
½ to 1 teaspoon red pepper flakes
235 g shredded Cheddar cheese or jalapeño Jack cheese

1. Preheat the air fryer to 200ºC. 2. In a baking tray, combine the water, grits, egg, butter, garlic, and red pepper flakes. Stir until well combined. 3. Stir in the shredded cheese. 4. Place the pan in the air fryer baskets and air fry for 12 minutes, or until the grits have cooked through and a knife inserted near the centre comes out clean. 5. Let stand for 5 minutes before serving.

Beetroot Salad with Lemon Vinaigrette

Prep time: 10 minutes | Cook time: 12 to 15 minutes | Serves 4

6 medium red and golden beetroots, peeled and sliced
1 teaspoon olive oil
¼ teaspoon rock salt
120 g crumbled feta cheese
2 kg mixed greens
Cooking spray
Vinaigrette:
2 teaspoons olive oil
2 tablespoons chopped fresh chives
Juice of 1 lemon

1. Preheat the air fryer to 180ºC. 2. In a large bowl, toss the beetroots, olive oil, and rock salt. 3. Spray the air fryer basket with cooking spray, then place the beetroots in the basket and air fry for 12 to 15 minutes or until tender. 4. While the beetroots cook, make the vinaigrette in a large bowl by whisking together the olive oil, lemon juice, and chives. 5. Remove the beetroots from the air fryer, toss in the vinaigrette, and allow to cool for 5 minutes. 6. Add the feta and serve on top of the mixed greens.

Easy Devils on Horseback

Prep time: 5 minutes | Cook time: 7 minutes | Serves 12

24 small pitted prunes (128 g)
60 g crumbled blue cheese, divided
8 slices centre-cut bacon, cut crosswise into thirds

1. Preheat the air fryer to 200ºC. 2. Halve the prunes lengthwise, but don't cut them all the way through. 3. Place ½ teaspoon of cheese in the centre of each prune. 4. Wrap a piece of bacon around each prune and secure the bacon with a toothpick. 5. Working in batches, arrange a single layer of the prunes in the air fryer baskets, half in zone 1 and the remaining in zone 2. 6. Air fry for about 7 minutes, flipping halfway, until the bacon is cooked through and crisp. 7. Let cool slightly and serve warm.

Baked Chorizo Scotch Eggs

Prep time: 5 minutes | Cook time: 15 to 20 minutes | Makes 4 eggs

450 g Mexican chorizo or other seasoned sausage meat
4 soft-boiled eggs plus 1 raw egg
1 tablespoon water
120 ml plain flour
235 ml panko breadcrumbs
Cooking spray

1. Divide the chorizo into 4 equal portions. Flatten each portion into a disc. Place a soft-boiled egg in the centre of each disc. Wrap the chorizo around the egg, encasing it completely. Place the encased eggs on a plate and chill for at least 30 minutes. 2. Preheat the air fryer to 180ºC. 3. Beat the raw egg with 1 tablespoon of water. Place the flour on a small plate and the panko on a second plate. Working with 1 egg at a time, roll the encased egg in the flour, then dip it in the egg mixture. Dredge the egg in the panko and place on a plate. Repeat with the remaining eggs. 4. Spray the eggs with oil and place in one of the air fryer baskets. Bake for 10 minutes. Turn and bake for an additional 5 to 10 minutes, or until browned and crisp on all sides. 5. Serve immediately.

Air Fried Broccoli & Simple Pea Delight

Prep time: 10 minutes | Cook time: 21 minutes

Air Fried Broccoli | Serves 1:

4 egg yolks
60 g melted butter
240 g coconut flour
Salt and pepper, to taste
475 g broccoli florets

Simple Pea Delight | Serves 2 to 4:

120 g flour
1 teaspoon baking powder
3 eggs
235 ml coconut milk
235 g soft white cheese
3 tablespoons pea protein
120 g chicken or turkey strips
Pinch of sea salt
235 g Mozzarella cheese

Prepare for Air Fried Broccoli:

1. Preheat the air fryer to 200ºC on zone 1 drawer.
2. In a bowl, whisk the egg yolks and melted butter together.
3. Throw in the coconut flour, salt and pepper, then stir again to combine well. 4. Dip each broccoli floret into the mixture and place in zone 1 drawer.

Prepare for Simple Pea Delight:

1. Preheat the air fryer to 200ºC on zone 2 drawer.
2. In a large bowl, mix all ingredients together using a large wooden spoon.
3. Place it in zone 2 drawer.

Cook:

1. In zone 1, set the temperature to 200ºC, set the time to 6 minutes. Work in batches if necessary.
2. In zone 2, set the temperature to 200ºC, set the time to 15 minutes.
3. Press SYNC, then press Start.
4. For Air Fried Broccoli, season with salt and pepper and serve with lemon wedges.

Air Fried Shishito Peppers

Prep time: 5 minutes | Cook time: 5 minutes | Serves 4

230 g shishito or Padron peppers (about 24)
1 tablespoon olive oil
Coarse sea salt, to taste
Lemon wedges, for serving
Cooking spray

1. Preheat the air fryer to 200ºC. 2. Spritz the air fryer basket with cooking spray. 3. Toss the peppers with olive oil in a large bowl to coat well. Arrange the peppers in the preheated air fryer. 4. Air fryer for 5 minutes or until blistered and lightly charred. Shake the basket and sprinkle the peppers with salt halfway through the cooking time. 5. Transfer the peppers onto a plate and squeeze the lemon wedges on top before serving.

Air Fried Tortilla Chips

Prep time: 5 minutes | Cook time: 10 minutes | Serves 4

4 six-inch corn tortillas, cut in half and slice into thirds
1 tablespoon rapeseed oil
¼ teaspoon rock salt
Cooking spray

1. Preheat the air fryer to 180ºC. 2. Spritz the air fryer basket with cooking spray. 3. On a clean work surface, brush the tortilla chips with rapeseed oil, then transfer the chips in the preheated air fryer. 4. Air fry for 10 minutes or until crunchy and lightly browned. 5. Shake the basket and sprinkle with salt halfway through the cooking time. 6. Transfer the chips onto a plate lined with paper towels. 7. Serve immediately.

Purple Potato Chips with Rosemary

Prep time: 10 minutes | Cook time: 9 to 14 minutes | Serves 6

235 ml Greek yoghurt
2 chipotle chillies, minced
2 tablespoons adobo or chipotle sauce
1 teaspoon paprika
1 tablespoon lemon juice
10 purple fingerling or miniature potatoes
1 teaspoon olive oil
2 teaspoons minced fresh rosemary leaves
⅛ teaspoon cayenne pepper
¼ teaspoon coarse sea salt

1. Preheat the air fryer to 200°C. 2. In a medium bowl, combine the yoghurt, minced chillies, adobo sauce, paprika, and lemon juice. Mix well and refrigerate. 3. Wash the potatoes and dry them with paper towels. 4. Slice the potatoes lengthwise, as thinly as possible. You can use a mandoline, a vegetable peeler, or a very sharp knife. 5. Combine the potato slices in a medium bowl and drizzle with the olive oil; toss to coat. 6. Put chips half in zone 1, the remaining in zone 2. In zone 1, set time to 9 to 14 minutes. In zone 2, select Match Cook and press Start. 7. Use tongs to gently rearrange the chips halfway during cooking time. 8. Sprinkle the chips with the rosemary, cayenne pepper, and sea salt. 9. Serve with the chipotle sauce for dipping.

Crunchy Fried Okra

Prep time: 5 minutes | Cook time: 8 to 10 minutes | Serves 4

120 g self-raising yellow cornmeal (alternatively add 1 tablespoon baking powder to cornmeal)
1 teaspoon Italian-style seasoning
1 teaspoon paprika
1 teaspoon salt
½ teaspoon freshly ground black pepper
2 large eggs, beaten
475 g okra slices
Cooking spray

1. Preheat the air fryer to 200°C. 2. Line the air fryer basket with parchment paper. In a shallow bowl, whisk the cornmeal, Italian-style seasoning, paprika, salt, and pepper until blended. 3. Place the beaten eggs in a second shallow bowl. Add the okra to the beaten egg and stir to coat. 4. Add the egg and okra mixture to the cornmeal mixture and stir until coated. 5. Place the okra on the parchment and spritz it with oil. 6. Air fry for 4 minutes. Shake the basket, spritz the okra with oil, and air fry for 4 to 6 minutes more until lightly browned and crispy. 7. Serve immediately.

Sweet Corn and Carrot Fritters

Prep time: 10 minutes | Cook time: 8 to 11 minutes | Serves 4

1 medium-sized carrot, grated
1 yellow onion, finely chopped
4 ounces (113 g) canned sweet corn kernels, drained
1 teaspoon sea salt flakes
1 tablespoon chopped fresh cilantro
1 medium-sized egg, whisked
2 tablespoons plain milk
1 cup grated Parmesan cheese
¼ cup flour
⅓ teaspoon baking powder
⅓ teaspoon sugar
Cooking spray

1. Preheat the air fryer to 180°C). 2. Place the grated carrot in a colander and press down to squeeze out any excess moisture. Dry it with a paper towel. 3. Combine the carrots with the remaining ingredients. 4. Mold 1 tablespoon of the mixture into a ball and press it down with your hand or a spoon to flatten it. Repeat until the rest of the mixture is used up. 5. Spritz the balls with cooking spray. 6. Arrange in the air fryer baskets, both zone 1 and zone 2, taking care not to overlap any balls. Bake for 8 to 11 minutes, or until they're firm. 7. Serve warm.

Herb-Roasted Veggies

Prep time: 10 minutes | Cook time: 14 to 18 minutes | Serves 4

1 red pepper, sliced
1 (230 g) package sliced mushrooms
235 g green beans, cut into 2-inch pieces
80 g diced red onion
3 garlic cloves, sliced
1 teaspoon olive oil
½ teaspoon dried basil
½ teaspoon dried tarragon

1. Preheat the air fryer to 180°C. 2. In a medium bowl, mix the red pepper, mushrooms, green beans, red onion, and garlic. 3. Drizzle with the olive oil. Toss to coat. 4. Add the herbs and toss again. Place the vegetables in one of the air fryer baskets. 5. Roast for 14 to 18 minutes, or until tender. 6. Serve immediately.

Easy Roasted Asparagus

Prep time: 5 minutes | Cook time: 6 minutes | Serves 4

450 g asparagus, trimmed and halved crosswise
1 teaspoon extra-virgin olive oil

Salt and pepper, to taste
Lemon wedges, for serving

1. Preheat the air fryer to 200°C. 2.Toss the asparagus with the oil, ⅛ teaspoon salt, and ⅛ teaspoon pepper in bowl. Transfer to air fryer basket. 3.Place the basket in air fryer and roast for 6 to 8 minutes, or until tender and bright green, tossing halfway through cooking. 4.Season with salt and pepper and serve with lemon wedges.

Scalloped Veggie Mix

Prep time: 10 minutes | Cook time: 15 minutes | Serves 4

1 Yukon Gold or other small white potato, thinly sliced
1 small sweet potato, peeled and thinly sliced
1 medium carrot, thinly sliced
60 g minced onion

3 garlic cloves, minced
180 ml 2 percent milk
2 tablespoons cornflour
½ teaspoon dried thyme

1. Preheat the air fryer to 190°C. 2. In a baking tray, layer the potato, sweet potato, carrot, onion, and garlic. 3. In a small bowl, whisk the milk, cornflour, and thyme until blended. 4. Pour the milk mixture evenly over the vegetables in the pan. Bake for 15 minutes. 5. Check the casserole—it should be golden brown on top, and the vegetables should be tender. 6. Serve immediately.

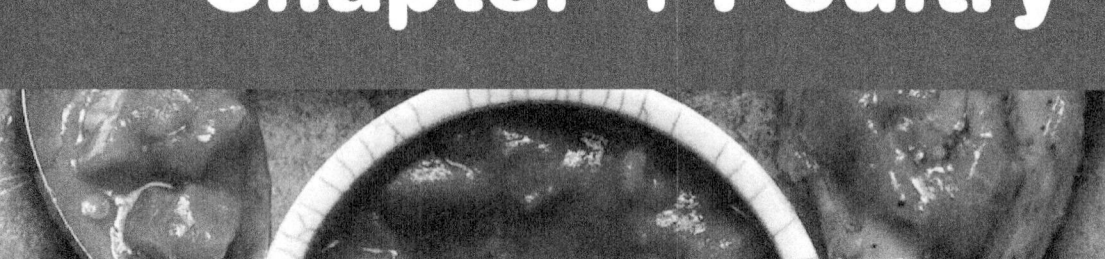

Chapter 4 Poultry

Chapter 4 Poultry

Brazilian Tempero Baiano Chicken Drumsticks

Prep time: 30 minutes | Cook time: 20 minutes | Serves 4

1 teaspoon cumin seeds	½ teaspoon black peppercorns
1 teaspoon dried oregano	½ teaspoon cayenne pepper
1 teaspoon dried parsley	60 ml fresh lime juice
1 teaspoon ground turmeric	2 tablespoons olive oil
½ teaspoon coriander seeds	680 g chicken drumsticks
1 teaspoon kosher salt	

1. In a clean coffee grinder or spice mill, combine the cumin, oregano, parsley, turmeric, coriander seeds, salt, peppercorns, and cayenne. Process until finely ground. 2. In a small bowl, combine the ground spices with the lime juice and oil. Place the chicken in a resealable plastic bag. Add the marinade, seal, and massage until the chicken is well coated. Marinate at room temperature for 30 minutes or in the refrigerator for up to 24 hours. 3. When you are ready to cook, place the drumsticks skin side up in zone 1 drawer. Set the air fryer to 200ºC for 20 to 25 minutes, turning the legs halfway through the cooking time. Use a meat thermometer to ensure that the chicken has reached an internal temperature of 76ºC. 4. Serve with plenty of napkins.

Korean Flavour Glazed Chicken Wings

Prep time: 10 minutes | Cook time: 25 minutes | Serves 4

Wings:

900 g chicken wings	1 tablespoon minced ginger
1 teaspoon salt	1 tablespoon minced garlic
1 teaspoon ground black pepper	1 teaspoon agave nectar
Sauce:	2 packets Splenda
2 tablespoons gochujang	1 tablespoon sesame oil
1 tablespoon mayonnaise	

For Garnish:

2 teaspoons sesame seeds	15 g chopped green onions

1. Preheat the air fryer to 200ºC. Line a baking pan with aluminum foil, then arrange the rack on the pan. 2. On a clean work surface, rub the chicken wings with salt and ground black pepper, then arrange the seasoned wings on the rack. 3. Air fry for 20 minutes or until the wings are well browned. Flip the wings halfway through. You may need to work in batches to avoid overcrowding. 4. Meanwhile, combine the ingredients for the sauce in a small bowl. Stir to mix well. Reserve half of the sauce in a separate bowl until ready to serve. 5. Remove the air fried chicken wings from the air fryer and toss with remaining half of the sauce to coat well. 6. Place the wings back to one of the air fryers and air fry for 5 more minutes or until the internal temperature of the wings reaches at least 76ºC. 7. Remove the wings from the air fryer and place on a large plate. Sprinkle with sesame seeds and green onions. Serve with reserved sauce.

Chicken and Avocado Fajitas

Prep time: 10 minutes | Cook time: 10 to 14 minutes | Serves 4

Cooking oil spray	dressing, divided
4 boneless, skinless chicken breasts, sliced crosswise	½ teaspoon dried oregano
	8 corn tortillas
1 small red onion, sliced	40 g torn butter lettuce leaves
2 red bell peppers, seeded and sliced	2 avocados, peeled, pitted, and chopped
120 ml spicy ranch salad	

1. Insert the crisper plate into one of the baskets and the basket into the unit. Preheat the unit by selecting BAKE, setting the temperature to 190ºC, and setting the time to 3 minutes. Select START/STOP to begin. 2. Once the unit is preheated, spray the crisper plate with cooking oil. Place the chicken, red onion, and red bell pepper into the basket. Drizzle with 1 tablespoon of the salad dressing and season with the oregano. Toss to combine. 3. Select BAKE, set the temperature to 190ºC, and set the time to 14 minutes. Select START/STOP to begin. 4. After 10 minutes, check the chicken. If a food thermometer inserted into the chicken registers at least 76ºC, it is done. If not, resume cooking. 5. When the cooking is complete, transfer the chicken and vegetables to a bowl and toss with the remaining salad dressing. 6. Serve the chicken mixture family-style with the tortillas, lettuce, and avocados, and let everyone make their own plates.

Turkey and Cranberry Quesadillas

Prep time: 7 minutes | Cook time: 4 to 8 minutes | Serves 4

6 low-sodium whole-wheat tortillas
75 g shredded low-sodium low-fat Swiss cheese
105 g shredded cooked low-sodium turkey breast
2 tablespoons cranberry sauce
2 tablespoons dried cranberries
½ teaspoon dried basil
Olive oil spray, for spraying the tortillas

1. Preheat the air fryer to 200°C. 2. Put 3 tortillas on a work surface. 3. Evenly divide the Swiss cheese, turkey, cranberry sauce, and dried cranberries among the tortillas. Sprinkle with the basil and top with the remaining tortillas. 4. Spray the outsides of the tortillas with olive oil spray. 5. One at a time, air fry the quesadillas in the air fryer for 4 to 8 minutes, or until crisp and the cheese is melted. Cut into quarters and serve.

French Garlic Chicken

Prep time: 30 minutes | Cook time: 27 minutes | Serves 4

2 tablespoon extra-virgin olive oil
1 tablespoon Dijon mustard
1 tablespoon apple cider vinegar
3 cloves garlic, minced
2 teaspoons herbes de Provence
½ teaspoon kosher salt
1 teaspoon black pepper
450 g boneless, skinless chicken thighs, halved crosswise
2 tablespoons butter
8 cloves garlic, chopped
60 g heavy whipping cream

1. In a small bowl, combine the olive oil, mustard, vinegar, minced garlic, herbes de Provence, salt, and pepper. Use a wire whisk to emulsify the mixture. 2. Pierce the chicken all over with a fork to allow the marinade to penetrate better. Place the chicken in a resealable plastic bag, pour the marinade over, and seal. Massage until the chicken is well coated. Marinate at room temperature for 30 minutes or in the refrigerator for up to 24 hours. 3. When you are ready to cook, place the butter and chopped garlic in a baking pan and place it in one of the air fryer baskets. Set the air fryer to 200°C for 5 minutes, or until the butter has melted and the garlic is sizzling. 4. Add the chicken and the marinade to the seasoned butter. Set the air fryer to 180°C for 15 minutes. Use a meat thermometer to ensure the chicken has reached an internal temperature of 76°C. Transfer the chicken to a plate and cover lightly with foil to keep warm. 5. Add the cream to the pan, stirring to combine with the garlic, butter, and cooking juices. Place the pan in the air fryer basket. Set the air fryer to 180°C for 7 minutes. 6. Pour the thickened sauce over the chicken and serve.

Jerk Chicken Thighs

Prep time: 30 minutes | Cook time: 15 to 20 minutes | Serves 6

2 teaspoons ground coriander
1 teaspoon ground allspice
1 teaspoon cayenne pepper
1 teaspoon ground ginger
1 teaspoon salt
1 teaspoon dried thyme
½ teaspoon ground cinnamon
½ teaspoon ground nutmeg
900 g boneless chicken thighs, skin on
2 tablespoons olive oil

1. In a small bowl, combine the coriander, allspice, cayenne, ginger, salt, thyme, cinnamon, and nutmeg. Stir until thoroughly combined. 2. Place the chicken in a baking dish and use paper towels to pat dry. Thoroughly coat both sides of the chicken with the spice mixture. Cover and refrigerate for at least 2 hours, preferably overnight. 3. Preheat the air fryer to 180°C. 4. Working in batches if necessary, arrange the chicken in a single layer half in zone 1 and the remaining in zone 2, and then lightly coat with the olive oil. In zone 1, select Air Fry button. In zone 2, select Match Cook and press Start. Pausing halfway through the cooking time to flip the chicken, air fry for 15 to 20 minutes, until a thermometer inserted into the thickest part registers 76°C.

Stuffed Turkey Roulade

Prep time: 10 minutes | Cook time: 45 minutes | Serves 4

1 (900 g) boneless turkey breast, skin removed
1 teaspoon salt
½ teaspoon black pepper
115 g goat cheese
1 tablespoon fresh thyme
1 tablespoon fresh sage
2 garlic cloves, minced
2 tablespoons olive oil
Fresh chopped parsley, for garnish

1. Preheat the air fryer to 190°C. 2. Using a sharp knife, butterfly the turkey breast, and season both sides with salt and pepper and set aside. 3. In a small bowl, mix together the goat cheese, thyme, sage, and garlic. 4. Spread the cheese mixture over the turkey breast, then roll it up tightly, tucking the ends underneath. 5. Place the turkey breast roulade onto a piece of aluminum foil, wrap it up, and place it into zone 1 drawer. 6. Bake for 30 minutes. Remove the foil from the turkey breast and brush the top with oil, then continue cooking for another 10 to 15 minutes, or until the outside has browned and the internal temperature reaches 76°C. 7. Remove and cut into 1-inch-wide slices and serve with a sprinkle of parsley on top.

Chicken Wings with Piri Piri Sauce

Prep time: 30 minutes | Cook time: 30 minutes | Serves 6

12 chicken wings
45 g butter, melted
1 teaspoon onion powder
½ teaspoon cumin powder
1 teaspoon garlic paste
Sauce:
60 g piri piri peppers, stemmed and chopped
1 tablespoon pimiento, seeded and minced
1 garlic clove, chopped
2 tablespoons fresh lemon juice
⅓ teaspoon sea salt
½ teaspoon tarragon

1. Steam the chicken wings using a steamer basket that is placed over a saucepan with boiling water; reduce the heat. 2. Now, steam the wings for 10 minutes over a moderate heat. Toss the wings with butter, onion powder, cumin powder, and garlic paste. 3. Let the chicken wings cool to room temperature. Then, refrigerate them for 45 to 50 minutes. 4. Roast in the preheated air fryer, pour them half in zone 1, the remaining in zone 2. In zone 1, select Air fry button, adjust temperature to 170, set time to 25 to 30 minutes. In zone 2, select Match Cook and press Start; make sure to flip them halfway through. 5. While the chicken wings are cooking, prepare the sauce by mixing all of the sauce ingredients in a food processor. Toss the wings with prepared Piri Piri Sauce and serve.

Indian Fennel Chicken

Prep time: 30 minutes | Cook time: 15 minutes | Serves 4

450 g boneless, skinless chicken thighs, cut crosswise into thirds
1 yellow onion, cut into 1½-inch-thick slices
1 tablespoon coconut oil, melted
2 teaspoons minced fresh ginger
2 teaspoons minced garlic
1 teaspoon smoked paprika
1 teaspoon ground fennel
1 teaspoon garam masala
1 teaspoon ground turmeric
1 teaspoon kosher salt
½ to 1 teaspoon cayenne pepper
Vegetable oil spray
2 teaspoons fresh lemon juice
5 g chopped fresh coriander or parsley

1. Use a fork to pierce the chicken all over to allow the marinade to penetrate better. 2. In a large bowl, combine the onion, coconut oil, ginger, garlic, paprika, fennel, garam masala, turmeric, salt, and cayenne. Add the chicken, toss to combine, and marinate at room temperature for 30 minutes, or cover and refrigerate for up to 24 hours. 3. Place the chicken and onion in one of the air fryer baskets. (Discard remaining marinade.) Spray with some vegetable oil spray. Set the air fryer to 180°C for 15 minutes. Halfway through the cooking time, remove the basket, spray the chicken and onion with more vegetable oil spray, and toss gently to coat. At the end of the cooking time, use a meat thermometer to ensure the chicken has reached an internal temperature of 76°C. 4. Transfer the chicken and onion to a serving platter. Sprinkle with the lemon juice and coriander and serve.

Bruschetta Chicken

Prep time: 10 minutes | Cook time: 20 minutes | Serves 4

Bruschetta Stuffing:

1 tomato, diced
3 tablespoons balsamic vinegar
1 teaspoon Italian seasoning
2 tablespoons chopped fresh basil
3 garlic cloves, minced
2 tablespoons extra-virgin olive oil

Chicken:

4 (115 g) boneless, skinless chicken breasts, cut 4 slits each
1 teaspoon Italian seasoning
Chicken seasoning or rub, to taste
Cooking spray

1. Preheat the air fryer to 190°. Spritz the air fryer basket with cooking spray. 2. Combine the ingredients for the bruschetta stuffing in a bowl. Stir to mix well. Set aside. 3. Rub the chicken breasts with Italian seasoning and chicken seasoning on a clean work surface. 4. Arrange the chicken breasts, slits side up, in a single layer in the air fryer basket and spritz with cooking spray. You may need to work in batches to avoid overcrowding, put them half in zone 1, and the remaining in zone 2. 5. Air fry for 7 minutes, then open the air fryer and fill the slits in the chicken with the bruschetta stuffing. Cook for another 3 minutes or until the chicken is well browned. 6. Serve immediately.

Apricot-Glazed Turkey Tenderloin

Prep time: 20 minutes | Cook time: 30 minutes | Serves 4

Olive oil
80 g sugar-free apricot preserves
½ tablespoon spicy brown mustard
680 g turkey breast tenderloin
Salt and freshly ground black pepper, to taste

1. Spray the air fryer basket lightly with olive oil. 2. In a small bowl, combine the apricot preserves and mustard to make a paste. 3. Season the turkey with salt and pepper. Spread the apricot paste all over the turkey. 4. Place the turkey in zone 1 drawer and lightly spray with olive oil. 5. Air fry at 190°C for 15 minutes. Flip the turkey over and lightly spray with olive oil. Air fry until the internal temperature reaches at least 76°C, an additional 10 to 15 minutes. 6. Let the turkey rest for 10 minutes before slicing and serving.

Chicken Parmesan

Prep time: 15 minutes | Cook time: 10 minutes | Serves 4

Oil, for spraying
2 (230 g) boneless, skinless chicken breasts
60 g Italian-style bread crumbs
20 g grated Parmesan cheese, plus 45 g shredded
4 tablespoons unsalted butter, melted
115 g marinara sauce

1. Preheat the air fryer to 180°C. Line the air fryer basket with parchment and spray lightly with oil. 2. Cut each chicken breast in half through its thickness to make 4 thin cutlets. Using a meat tenderizer, pound each cutlet until it is about ¾ inch thick. 3. On a plate, mix together the bread crumbs and grated Parmesan cheese. 4. Lightly brush the chicken with the melted butter, then dip into the bread crumb mixture. 5. Place the chicken in the prepared baskets and spray lightly with oil. You may need to work in batches, depending on the size of your air fryer. 6. Cook for 6 minutes. Top the chicken with the marinara and shredded Parmesan cheese, dividing evenly. Cook for another 3 to 4 minutes, or until golden brown, crispy, and the internal temperature reaches 76°C.

Stuffed Chicken Florentine

Prep time: 10 minutes | Cook time: 20 minutes | Serves 4

3 tablespoons pine nuts
40 g frozen spinach, thawed and squeezed dry
75 g ricotta cheese
2 tablespoons grated Parmesan cheese
3 cloves garlic, minced
Salt and freshly ground black pepper, to taste
4 small boneless, skinless chicken breast halves (about 680 g)
8 slices bacon

1. Place the pine nuts in a small pan and set in the air fryer basket. Set the air fryer to 200°C and air fry for 2 to 3 minutes until toasted. Remove the pine nuts to a mixing bowl and continue preheating the air fryer. 2. In a large bowl, combine the spinach, ricotta, Parmesan, and garlic. Season to taste with salt and pepper and stir well until thoroughly combined. 3. Using a sharp knife, cut into the chicken breasts, slicing them across and opening them up like a book, but be careful not to cut them all the way through. Sprinkle the chicken with salt and pepper. 4. Spoon equal amounts of the spinach mixture into the chicken, then fold the top of the chicken breast back over the top of the stuffing. Wrap each chicken breast with 2 slices of bacon. 5. Working in batches if necessary, put chicken half in zone 1 and the remaining in zone 2, air fry the chicken for 18 to 20 minutes until the bacon is crisp and a thermometer inserted into the thickest part of the chicken registers 76°C.

Honey-Glazed Chicken Thighs

Prep time: 5 minutes | Cook time: 14 minutes | Serves 4

Oil, for spraying
4 boneless, skinless chicken thighs, fat trimmed
3 tablespoons soy sauce
1 tablespoon balsamic vinegar
2 teaspoons honey
2 teaspoons minced garlic
1 teaspoon ground ginger

1. Preheat the air fryer to 200°C. Line one of the air fryer baskets with parchment and spray lightly with oil. 2. Place the chicken in the prepared basket. 3. Cook for 7 minutes, flip, and cook for another 7 minutes, or until the internal temperature reaches 76°C and the juices run clear. 4. In a small saucepan, combine the soy sauce, balsamic vinegar, honey, garlic, and ginger and cook over low heat for 1 to 2 minutes, until warmed through. 5. Transfer the chicken to a serving plate and drizzle with the sauce just before serving.

Sweet and Spicy Turkey Meatballs

Prep time: 15 minutes | Cook time: 15 minutes | Serves 6

Olive oil
450 g lean turkey mince
30 g whole-wheat panko bread crumbs
1 egg, beaten
1 tablespoon soy sauce
60 ml plus 1 tablespoon hoisin sauce, divided
2 teaspoons minced garlic
⅛ teaspoon salt
⅛ teaspoon freshly ground black pepper
1 teaspoon Sriracha

1. Spray the air fryer basket lightly with olive oil. 2. In a large bowl, mix together the turkey, panko bread crumbs, egg, soy sauce, 1 tablespoon of hoisin sauce, garlic, salt, and black pepper. 3. Using a tablespoon, form 24 meatballs. 4. In a small bowl, combine the remaining 60 ml of hoisin sauce and Sriracha to make a glaze and set aside. 5. Place the meatballs half in zone 1, the remaining in zone 2 in a single layer. You may need to cook them in batches. 6. In zone 1, select Air fry button, adjust temperature to 180, set time to 8 minutes. In zone 2, select Match Cook and press Start. Brush the meatballs generously with the glaze and cook until cooked through, an additional 4 to 7 minutes.

Greek Chicken Souvlaki

Prep time: 30 minutes | Cook time: 15 minutes | Serves 3 to 4

Chicken:

Grated zest and juice of 1 lemon
2 tablespoons extra-virgin olive oil
1 tablespoon Greek souvlaki seasoning
450 g boneless, skinless chicken breast, cut into 2-inch chunks
Vegetable oil spray

For Serving:

Warm pita bread or hot cooked rice
Sliced ripe tomatoes
Sliced cucumbers
Thinly sliced red onion
Kalamata olives
Tzatziki

1. For the chicken: In a small bowl, combine the lemon zest, lemon juice, olive oil, and souvlaki seasoning. Place the chicken in a gallon-size resealable plastic bag. Pour the marinade over chicken. Seal bag and massage to coat. Place the bag in a large bowl and marinate for 30 minutes, or cover and refrigerate up to 24 hours, turning the bag occasionally. 2. Place the chicken a single layer in one of the air fryer baskets. Set the air fryer to 180°C for 10 minutes, turning the chicken and spraying with a little vegetable oil spray halfway through the cooking time. Increase the air fryer temperature to 200°C for 5 minutes to allow the chicken to crisp and brown a little. 3. Transfer the chicken to a serving platter and serve with pita bread or rice, tomatoes, cucumbers, onion, olives and tzatziki.

Chicken Chimichangas

Prep time: 20 minutes | Cook time: 8 to 10 minutes | Serves 4

280 g cooked chicken, shredded
2 tablespoons chopped green chilies
½ teaspoon oregano
½ teaspoon cumin
½ teaspoon onion powder
¼ teaspoon garlic powder
Salt and pepper, to taste
8 flour tortillas (6- or 7-inch diameter)
Oil for misting or cooking spray
Chimichanga Sauce:
2 tablespoons butter
2 tablespoons flour
235 ml chicken broth
60 g light sour cream
¼ teaspoon salt
60 g Pepper Jack or Monterey Jack cheese, shredded

1. Make the sauce by melting butter in a saucepan over medium-low heat. Stir in flour until smooth and slightly bubbly. Gradually add broth, stirring constantly until smooth. Cook and stir 1 minute, until the mixture slightly thickens. Remove from heat and stir in sour cream and salt. Set aside. 2. In a medium bowl, mix together the chicken, chilies, oregano, cumin, onion powder, garlic, salt, and pepper. Stir in 3 to 4 tablespoons of the sauce, using just enough to make the filling moist but not soupy. 3. Divide filling among the 8 tortillas. Place filling down the centre of tortilla, stopping about 1 inch from edges. Fold one side of tortilla over filling, fold the two sides in, and then roll up. Mist all sides with oil or cooking spray. 4. Place chimichangas in air fryer baskets seam side down. To fit more into the basket, you can stand them on their sides with the seams against the sides of the basket. 5. Air fry at 180°C for 8 to 10 minutes or until heated through and crispy brown outside. 6. Add the shredded cheese to the remaining sauce. Stir over low heat, warming just until the cheese melts. Don't boil or sour cream may curdle. 7. Drizzle the sauce over the chimichangas.

Chicken Breasts with Asparagus, Beans, and Rocket

Prep time: 20 minutes | Cook time: 25 minutes | Serves 2

160 g canned cannellini beans, rinsed
1½ tablespoons red wine vinegar
1 garlic clove, minced
2 tablespoons extra-virgin olive oil, divided
Salt and ground black pepper, to taste
½ red onion, sliced thinly
230 g asparagus, trimmed and cut into 1-inch lengths
2 (230 g) boneless, skinless chicken breasts, trimmed
¼ teaspoon paprika
½ teaspoon ground coriander
60 g baby rocket, rinsed and drained

1. Preheat the air fryer to 200°C. 2. Warm the beans in microwave for 1 minutes and combine with red wine vinegar, garlic, 1 tablespoon of olive oil, ¼ teaspoon of salt, and ¼ teaspoon of ground black pepper in a bowl. Stir to mix well. 3. Combine the onion with ⅛ teaspoon of salt, ⅛ teaspoon of ground black pepper, and 2 teaspoons of olive oil in a separate bowl. Toss to coat well. 4. Place the onion in zone 1 drawer and air fry for 2 minutes, then add the asparagus and air fry for 8 more minutes or until the asparagus is tender. Shake the basket halfway through. Transfer the onion and asparagus to the bowl with beans. Set aside. 5. Toss the chicken breasts with remaining ingredients, except for the baby rocket, in a large bowl. 6. Put the chicken breasts in zone 1 drawer and air fry for 14 minutes or until the internal temperature of the chicken reaches at least 76°C. Flip the breasts halfway through. 7. Remove the chicken from the air fryer and serve on an aluminum foil with asparagus, beans, onion, and rocket. Sprinkle with salt and ground black pepper. Toss to serve.

Curried Orange Honey Chicken

Prep time: 10 minutes | Cook time: 16 to 19 minutes | Serves 4

340 g boneless, skinless chicken thighs, cut into 1-inch pieces
1 yellow bell pepper, cut into 1½-inch pieces
1 small red onion, sliced
Olive oil for misting
60 ml chicken stock
2 tablespoons honey
60 ml orange juice
1 tablespoon cornflour
2 to 3 teaspoons curry powder

1. Preheat the air fryer to 190ºC. 2. Put the chicken thighs, pepper, and red onion in one of the air fryer baskets and mist with olive oil. 3. Roast for 12 to 14 minutes or until the chicken is cooked to 76ºC, shaking the basket halfway through cooking time. 4. Remove the chicken and vegetables from the air fryer basket and set aside. 5. In a metal bowl, combine the stock, honey, orange juice, cornflour, and curry powder, and mix well. Add the chicken and vegetables, stir, and put the bowl in the basket. 6. Return the basket to the air fryer and roast for 2 minutes. Remove and stir, then roast for 2 to 3 minutes or until the sauce is thickened and bubbly. 7. Serve warm.

Coconut Chicken Wings with Mango Sauce

Prep time: 15 minutes | Cook time: 20 minutes | Serves 4

16 chicken drumettes (party wings)
60 ml full-fat coconut milk
1 tablespoon sriracha
1 teaspoon onion powder
1 teaspoon garlic powder
Salt and freshly ground black pepper, to taste
25 g shredded unsweetened coconut
30 g all-purpose flour
Cooking oil spray
165 g mango, cut into ½-inch chunks
15 g fresh coriander, chopped
25 g red onion, chopped
2 garlic cloves, minced
Juice of ½ lime

1. Place the drumettes in a resealable plastic bag. 2. In a small bowl, whisk the coconut milk and sriracha. 3. Drizzle the drumettes with the sriracha–coconut milk mixture. Season the drumettes with the onion powder, garlic powder, salt, and pepper. Seal the bag. Shake it thoroughly to combine the seasonings and coat the chicken. Marinate for at least 30 minutes, preferably overnight, in the refrigerator. 4. When the drumettes are almost done marinating, in a large bowl, stir together the shredded coconut and flour. 5. Dip the drumettes into the coconut-flour mixture. Press the flour mixture onto the chicken with your hands. 6. Insert the crisper plate into one of the baskets and the basket into the unit. Preheat the unit by selecting AIR FRY, setting the temperature to 200ºC, and setting the time to 3 minutes. Select START/STOP to begin. 7. Once the unit is preheated, spray the crisper plate and the basket with cooking oil. Place the drumettes in the air fryer. It is okay to stack them. Spray the drumettes with cooking oil, being sure to cover the bottom layer. 8. Select AIR FRY, set the temperature to 200ºC, and set the time to 20 minutes. Select START/STOP to begin. 9. After 5 minutes, remove the basket and shake it to ensure all pieces cook through. Reinsert the basket to resume cooking. Remove and shake the basket every 5 minutes, twice more, until a food thermometer inserted into the drumettes registers 76ºC. 10. When the cooking is complete, let the chicken cool for 5 minutes. 11. While the chicken cooks and cools, make the salsa. In a small bowl, combine the mango, coriander, red onion, garlic, and lime juice. Mix well until fully combined. Serve with the wings.

Italian Crispy Chicken

Prep time: 10 minutes | Cook time: 20 minutes | Serves 4

2 (115 g) boneless, skinless chicken breasts
2 egg whites, beaten
60 g Italian bread crumbs
45 g grated Parmesan cheese
2 teaspoons Italian seasoning
Salt and freshly ground black pepper, to taste
Cooking oil spray
180 g marinara sauce
110 g shredded Mozzarella cheese

1. With your knife blade parallel to the cutting board, cut the chicken breasts in half horizontally to create 4 thin cutlets. On a solid surface, pound the cutlets to flatten them. You can use your hands, a rolling pin, a kitchen mallet, or a meat hammer. 2. Pour the egg whites into a bowl large enough to dip the chicken. 3. In another bowl large enough to dip a chicken cutlet in, stir together the bread crumbs, Parmesan cheese, and Italian seasoning, and season with salt and pepper. 4. Dip each cutlet into the egg whites and into the breadcrumb mixture to coat. 5. Insert the crisper plate into the basket and the basket into the unit. Preheat the unit by selecting AIR FRY, setting the temperature to 190ºC, and setting the time to 3 minutes. Select START/STOP to begin. 6. Once the unit is preheated, spray the crisper plate with cooking oil. Working in batches, place chicken cutlets half in zone 1 drawer, the remaining in zone 2 drawer. Spray the top of the chicken with cooking oil. 7. In zone 1, Select AIR FRY, set the temperature to 190ºC, and set the time to 7 minutes. In zone 2, select Match Cook and press Start. 8. When the cooking is complete, repeat steps 6 and 7 with the remaining cutlets. 9. Top the chicken cutlets with the marinara sauce and shredded Mozzarella cheese. 10. The cooking is complete when the cheese is melted and the chicken reaches an internal temperature of 76ºC. Cool for 5 minutes before serving.

Tex-Mex Chicken Roll-Ups

Prep time: 10 minutes | Cook time: 14 to 17 minutes | Serves 8

900 g boneless, skinless chicken breasts or thighs	black pepper, to taste
1 teaspoon chili powder	170 g Monterey Jack cheese, shredded
½ teaspoon smoked paprika	115 g canned diced green chilies
½ teaspoon ground cumin	Avocado oil spray
Sea salt and freshly ground	

1. Place the chicken in a large zip-top bag or between two pieces of plastic wrap. Using a meat mallet or heavy skillet, pound the chicken until it is about ¼ inch thick. 2. In a small bowl, combine the chili powder, smoked paprika, cumin, and salt and pepper to taste. Sprinkle both sides of the chicken with the seasonings. 3. Sprinkle the chicken with the Monterey Jack cheese, then the diced green chilies. 4. Roll up each piece of chicken from the long side, tucking in the ends as you go. Secure the roll-up with a toothpick. 5. Set the air fryer to 180ºC. . Spray the outside of the chicken with avocado oil. Place the chicken in a single layer half in zone 1 drawer, the remaining in zone 2 drawer, working in batches if necessary, and roast for 7 minutes. Flip and cook for another 7 to 10 minutes, until an instant-read thermometer reads 70ºC. 6. Remove the chicken from the air fryer and allow it to rest for about 5 minutes before serving.

Korean Honey Wings

Prep time: 10 minutes | Cook time: 25 minutes per batch | Serves 4

55 g gochujang, or red pepper paste	2 teaspoons ground ginger
55 g mayonnaise	1.4 kg whole chicken wings
2 tablespoons honey	Olive oil spray
1 tablespoon sesame oil	1 teaspoon salt
2 teaspoons minced garlic	½ teaspoon freshly ground black pepper
1 tablespoon sugar	

1. In a large bowl, whisk the gochujang, mayonnaise, honey, sesame oil, garlic, sugar, and ginger. Set aside. 2. Insert the crisper plate into the basket and the basket into the unit. Preheat the unit by selecting AIR FRY, setting the temperature to 200ºC, and setting the time to 3 minutes. Select START/STOP to begin. 3. To prepare the chicken wings, cut the wings in half. The meatier part is the drumette. Cut off and discard the wing tip from the flat part (or save the wing tips in the freezer to make chicken stock). 4. Once the unit is preheated, spray the crisper plate with olive oil. Working in batches, place half the chicken wings in zone 1, the remaining in zone 2, spray them with olive oil, and sprinkle with the salt and pepper. 5. In zone 1, select Air Fry button, adjust temperature to 200, set time to 20 minutes. In zone 2, select Match Cook and press Start. 6. After 10 minutes, remove the basket, flip the wings, and spray them with more olive oil. Reinsert the basket to resume cooking. 7. Cook the wings to an internal temperature of 76ºC, then transfer them to the bowl with the prepared sauce and toss to coat. 8. Repeat steps 4, 5, 6, and 7 for the remaining chicken wings. 9. Return the coated wings to the basket and air fry for 4 to 6 minutes more until the sauce has glazed the wings and the chicken is crisp. After 3 minutes, check the wings to make sure they aren't burning. Serve hot.

Hawaiian Huli Huli Chicken

Prep time: 30 minutes | Cook time: 15 minutes | Serves 4

4 boneless, skinless chicken thighs (680 g)	25 g sugar
1 (230 g) can pineapple chunks in juice, drained, 60 ml juice reserved	2 tablespoons ketchup
	1 tablespoon minced fresh ginger
	1 tablespoon minced garlic
60 ml soy sauce	25 g chopped spring onions

1. Use a fork to pierce the chicken all over to allow the marinade to penetrate better. Place the chicken in a large bowl or large resealable plastic bag. 2. Set the drained pineapple chunks aside. In a small microwave-safe bowl, combine the pineapple juice, soy sauce, sugar, ketchup, ginger, and garlic. Pour half the sauce over the chicken; toss to coat. Reserve the remaining sauce. Marinate the chicken at room temperature for 30 minutes, or cover and refrigerate for up to 24 hours. 3. Place the chicken in one of the air fryer baskets. (Discard marinade.) Set the air fryer to 180ºC for 15 minutes, turning halfway through the cooking time. 4. Meanwhile, microwave the reserved sauce on high for 45 to 60 seconds, stirring every 15 seconds, until the sauce has the consistency of a thick glaze. 5. At the end of the cooking time, use a meat thermometer to ensure the chicken has reached an internal temperature of 76ºC. 6. Transfer the chicken to a serving platter. Pour the sauce over the chicken. Garnish with the pineapple chunks and spring onions.

Chicken Enchiladas

Prep time: 10 minutes | Cook time: 8 minutes | Serves 4

Oil, for spraying
420 g shredded cooked chicken
1 package taco seasoning
8 flour tortillas, at room temperature
60 g canned black beans, rinsed and drained

1 (115 g) can diced green chilies, drained
1 (280 g) can red or green enchilada sauce
235 g shredded Cheddar cheese

1. Line the air fryer basket with parchment and spray lightly with oil. (Do not skip the step of lining the basket; the parchment will keep the sauce and cheese from dripping through the holes.) 2. In a small bowl, mix together the chicken and taco seasoning. 3. Divide the mixture among the tortillas. Top with the black beans and green chilis. Carefully roll up each tortilla. 4. Place the enchiladas, seam-side down, in two prepared baskets. You may need to work in batches, depending on the size of your air fryer. 5. Spoon the enchilada sauce over the enchiladas. Use just enough sauce to keep them from drying out. You can add more sauce when serving. Sprinkle the cheese on top. 6. Air fry at 180ºC for 5 to 8 minutes, or until heated through and the cheese is melted. 7. Place 2 enchiladas on each plate and top with more enchilada sauce, if desired.

Chapter 5 Fish and Seafood

Chapter 5 Fish and Seafood

Seasoned Breaded Prawns

Prep time: 15 minutes | Cook time: 10 to 15 minutes | Serves 4

2 teaspoons Old Bay seasoning, divided
½ teaspoon garlic powder
½ teaspoon onion powder
455 g large prawns, peeled and deveined, with tails on
2 large eggs
40 g whole-wheat panko bread crumbs
Cooking spray

1. Preheat the air fryer to 190ºC. 2. Spray the air fryer baskets lightly with cooking spray. 3. In a medium bowl, mix together 1 teaspoon of Old Bay seasoning, garlic powder, and onion powder. Add the prawns and toss with the seasoning mix to lightly coat. 4. In a separate small bowl, whisk the eggs with 1 teaspoon water. 5. In a shallow bowl, mix together the remaining 1 teaspoon Old Bay seasoning and the panko bread crumbs. 6. Dip each prawns in the egg mixture and dredge in the bread crumb mixture to evenly coat. 7. Place the prawns in two air fryer baskets, in a single layer. Lightly spray the prawns with cooking spray. You many need to cook the prawns in batches. 8. Air fry for 10 to 15 minutes, or until the prawns is cooked through and crispy, shaking the basket at 5-minute intervals to redistribute and evenly cook. 9. Serve immediately.

Roasted Cod with Lemon-Garlic Potatoes

Prep time: 10 minutes | Cook time: 28 minutes | Serves 2

3 tablespoons unsalted butter, softened, divided
2 garlic cloves, minced
1 lemon, grated to yield 2 teaspoons zest and sliced ¼ inch thick
Salt and pepper, to taste
1 large russet potato (about 340 g), unpeeled, sliced ¼ inch thick
1 tablespoon minced fresh parsley, chives, or tarragon
2 (230 g) skinless cod fillets, 1¼ inches thick
Vegetable oil spray

1. Preheat the air fryer to 200ºC. 2. Make foil sling for air fryer basket by folding 1 long sheet of aluminum foil so it is 4 inches wide. Lay sheet of foil widthwise across basket, pressing foil into and up sides of basket. Fold excess foil as needed so that edges of foil are flush with top of basket. Lightly spray the foil and basket with vegetable oil spray. 3. Microwave 1 tablespoon butter, garlic, 1 teaspoon lemon zest, ¼ teaspoon salt, and ⅛ teaspoon pepper in a medium bowl, stirring once, until the butter is melted and the mixture is fragrant, about 30 seconds. Add the potato slices and toss to coat. Shingle the potato slices on sling in prepared basket to create 2 even layers. Air fry until potato slices are spotty brown and just tender, 16 to 18 minutes, using a sling to rotate potatoes halfway through cooking. 4. Combine the remaining 2 tablespoons butter, remaining 1 teaspoon lemon zest, and parsley in a small bowl. Pat the cod dry with paper towels and season with salt and pepper. Place the fillets, skinned-side down, on top of potato slices, spaced evenly apart. (Tuck thinner tail ends of fillets under themselves as needed to create uniform pieces.) Dot the fillets with the butter mixture and top with the lemon slices. Return the basket to the air fryer and air fry until the cod flakes apart when gently prodded with a paring knife and registers 60ºC, 12 to 15 minutes, using a sling to rotate the potato slices and cod halfway through cooking. 5. Using a sling, carefully remove potatoes and cod from air fryer. Cut the potato slices into 2 portions between fillets using fish spatula. Slide spatula along underside of potato slices and transfer with cod to individual plates. Serve.

Crab-Stuffed Avocado Boats

Prep time: 5 minutes | Cook time: 7 minutes | Serves 4

2 medium avocados, halved and pitted
230 g cooked crab meat
¼ teaspoon Old Bay seasoning
2 tablespoons peeled and diced yellow onion
2 tablespoons mayonnaise

1. Scoop out avocado flesh in each avocado half, leaving ½ inch around edges to form a shell. Chop scooped-out avocado. 2. In a medium bowl, combine crab meat, Old Bay seasoning, onion, mayonnaise, and chopped avocado. Place ¼ mixture into each avocado shell. 3. Place avocado boats into one of the ungreased air fryer baskets. Adjust the temperature to 180ºC and air fry for 7 minutes. Avocado will be browned on the top and mixture will be bubbling when done. Serve warm.

Salmon with Fennel and Carrot

Prep time: 15 minutes | Cook time: 15 minutes | Serves 4

1 fennel bulb, thinly sliced
2 large carrots, sliced
1 large onion, thinly sliced
2 teaspoons extra-virgin olive oil
120 ml sour cream
1 teaspoon dried tarragon leaves
4 (140 g) salmon fillets
⅛ teaspoon salt
¼ teaspoon coarsely ground black pepper

1. Insert the crisper plate into one of the baskets and the basket into the unit. Preheat the unit to 200ºC, 2. In a medium bowl, toss together the fennel, carrots, and onion. Add the olive oil and toss again to coat the vegetables. Put the vegetables into a 6-inch round metal pan. 3. Once the unit is preheated, place the pan into the basket. 4. Cook for 15 minutes. 5. Check after 5 minutes, the vegetables should be crisp-tender. Remove the pan and stir in the sour cream and tarragon. Top with the salmon fillets and sprinkle the fish with the salt and pepper. Reinsert the pan into the basket and resume cooking. 6. When the cooking is complete, the salmon should flake easily with a fork and a food thermometer should register at least 64ºC. Serve the salmon on top of the vegetables.

Tortilla Prawn Tacos

Prep time: 10 minutes | Cook time: 6 minutes | Serves 4

Spicy Mayo:
3 tablespoons mayonnaise
1 tablespoon Louisiana-style hot pepper sauce, or Sriracha

Coriander-Lime Slaw:
180 g shredded green cabbage
½ small red onion, thinly sliced
1 small jalapeño, thinly sliced
2 tablespoons chopped fresh cilantro
Juice of 1 lime
¼ teaspoon kosher salt
Prawns:
1 large egg, beaten
1 cup crushed tortilla chips
24 jumbo prawns (about 455 g), peeled and deveined
⅛ teaspoon kosher or coarse sea salt
Cooking spray
8 corn tortillas, for serving

1. For the spicy mayo: In a small bowl, mix the mayonnaise and hot pepper sauce. 2. For the coriander-lime slaw: In a large bowl, toss together the cabbage, onion, jalapeño, coriander, lime juice, and salt to combine. Cover and refrigerate to chill. 3. For the prawns: Place the egg in a shallow bowl and the crushed tortilla chips in another. Season the prawns with the salt. Dip the prawns in the egg, then in the crumbs, pressing gently to adhere. Place on a work surface and spray both sides with oil. 4. Preheat the air fryer to 180ºC. 5. Working in batches, arrange a single layer of the prawns in the air fryer baskets. Air fry for 6 minutes, flipping halfway, until golden and cooked through in the center. 6. To serve, place 2 tortillas on each plate and top each with 3 prawns. Top each taco with ¼ of the slaw, then drizzle with spicy mayo.

Parmesan-Crusted Halibut Fillets

Prep time: 5 minutes | Cook time: 10 minutes | Serves 4

2 medium-sized halibut fillets
Dash of tabasco sauce
1 teaspoon curry powder
½ teaspoon ground coriander
½ teaspoon hot paprika
Kosher or coarse sea salt, and freshly cracked mixed peppercorns, to taste
2 eggs
1½ tablespoons olive oil
75 g grated Parmesan cheese

1. Preheat the air fryer to 190ºC. 2. On a clean work surface, drizzle the halibut fillets with the tabasco sauce. Sprinkle with the curry powder, coriander, hot paprika, salt, and cracked mixed peppercorns. Set aside. 3. In a shallow bowl, beat the eggs until frothy. In another shallow bowl, combine the olive oil and Parmesan cheese. 4. One at a time, dredge the halibut fillets in the beaten eggs, shaking off any excess, then roll them over the Parmesan cheese until evenly coated. 5. Arrange the halibut fillets in the air fryer basket in a single layer and air fry for 10 minutes, or until the fish is golden brown and crisp. 6. Cool for 5 minutes before serving.

Pecan-Crusted Catfish

Prep time: 5 minutes | Cook time: 12 minutes | Serves 4

65 g pecans, finely crushed
1 teaspoon fine sea salt
¼ teaspoon ground black pepper
4 catfish fillets, 110g each
For Garnish (Optional):
Fresh oregano
Pecan halves

1. Spray the air fryer basket with avocado oil. Preheat the air fryer to 190ºC. 2. In a large bowl, mix the crushed pecan, salt, and pepper. One at a time, dredge the catfish fillets in the mixture, coating them well. Use your hands to press the pecan meal into the fillets. Spray the fish with avocado oil and place them in one of the air fryer baskets. 3. Air fry the coated catfish for 12 minutes, or until it flakes easily and is no longer translucent in the center, flipping halfway through. 4. Garnish with oregano sprigs and pecan halves, if desired. 5. Store leftovers in an airtight container in the fridge for up to 3 days. Reheat in a preheated 180ºC air fryer for 4 minutes, or until heated through.

Sole and Cauliflower Fritters

Prep time: 5 minutes | Cook time: 24 minutes | Serves 2

230 g sole fillets
230 g mashed cauliflower
75 g red onion, chopped
1 bell pepper, finely chopped
1 egg, beaten
2 garlic cloves, minced
2 tablespoons fresh parsley, chopped
1 tablespoon olive oil
1 tablespoon coconut aminos or tamari
½ teaspoon scotch bonnet pepper, minced
½ teaspoon paprika
Salt and white pepper, to taste
Cooking spray

1. Preheat the air fryer to 200ºC. Spray one of the air fryer baskets with cooking spray. 2. Place the sole fillets in the basket and air fry for 10 minutes, flipping them halfway through. 3. When the fillets are done, transfer them to a large bowl. Mash the fillets into flakes. Add the remaining ingredients and stir to combine. 4. Make the fritters: Scoop out 2 tablespoons of the fish mixture and shape into a patty about ½ inch thick with your hands. Repeat with the remaining fish mixture. 5. Arrange the patties in the air fryer basket and bake for 14 minutes, flipping the patties halfway through, or until they are golden brown and cooked through. 6. Cool for 5 minutes and serve on a plate.

Pesto Fish Pie

Prep time: 15 minutes | Cook time: 15 minutes | Serves 4

2 tablespoons prepared pesto
60 ml single cream
20 g grated Parmesan cheese
1 teaspoon kosher or coarse sea salt
1 teaspoon black pepper
Vegetable oil spray
280 g frozen chopped spinach, thawed and squeezed dry
455 g firm white fish, cut into 2-inch chunks
115 g cherry tomatoes, quartered
Plain flour
½ sheet frozen puff pastry (from a 490 g package), thawed

1. In a small bowl, combine the pesto, single cream, Parmesan, salt, and pepper. Stir until well combined; set aside. 2. Spray a baking pan with vegetable oil spray. Arrange the spinach evenly across the bottom of the pan. Top with the fish and tomatoes. Pour the pesto mixture evenly over everything. 3. On a lightly floured surface, roll the puff pastry sheet into a circle. Place the pastry on top of the pan and tuck it in around the edges of the pan. (Or, do what I do and stretch it with your hands and then pat it into place.) 4. Place the pan in one of the air fryer baskets. Set the air fryer to 200ºC for 15 minutes, or until the pastry is well browned. Let stand 5 minutes before serving.

Classic Prawns Empanadas

Prep time: 10 minutes | Cook time: 8 minutes | Serves 5

230 g raw prawns, peeled, deveined and chopped
1 small chopped red onion
1 spring onion, chopped
2 garlic cloves, minced
2 tablespoons minced red bell pepper
2 tablespoons chopped fresh coriander
½ tablespoon fresh lime juice
¼ teaspoon sweet paprika
⅛ teaspoon kosher salt
⅛ teaspoon crushed red pepper flakes (optional)
1 large egg, beaten
10 frozen Goya Empanada Discos, thawed
Cooking spray

1. In a medium bowl, combine the prawns, red onion, spring onion, garlic, bell pepper, coriander, lime juice, paprika, salt, and pepper flakes (if using). 2. In a small bowl, beat the egg with 1 teaspoon water until smooth. 3. Place an empanada disc on a work surface and put 2 tablespoons of the prawn mixture in the center. Brush the outer edges of the disc with the egg wash. Fold the disc over and gently press the edges to seal. Use a fork and press around the edges to crimp and seal completely. Brush the tops of the empanadas with the egg wash. 4. Preheat the air fryer to 190ºC. 5. Spray the bottom of the 2 air fryer baskets with cooking spray to prevent sticking, put the empanadas half in zone 1, and the remaining in zone 2. Working in batches if necessary, arrange a single layer of the empanadas in the air fryer basket and air fry for about 8 minutes, flipping halfway, until golden brown and crispy. 6. Serve hot.

Sole Fillets

Prep time: 10 minutes | Cook time: 5 to 8 minutes | Serves 4

1 egg white
1 tablespoon water
30 g panko breadcrumbs
2 tablespoons extra-light virgin olive oil
4 sole fillets, 110 g each
Salt and pepper, to taste
Olive or vegetable oil for misting or cooking spray

1. Preheat the air fryer to 390ºF (200ºC). 2. Beat together egg white and water in shallow dish. 3. In another shallow dish, mix panko crumbs and oil until well combined and crumbly (best done by hand). 4. Season sole fillets with salt and pepper to taste. Dip each fillet into egg mixture and then roll in panko crumbs, pressing in crumbs so that fish is nicely coated. 5. Spray one of the air fryer baskets with nonstick cooking spray and add fillets. Air fry at 200ºC for 3 minutes. 6. Spray fish fillets but do not turn. Cook 2 to 5 minutes longer or until golden brown and crispy. Using a spatula, carefully remove fish from basket and serve.

Crunchy Fish Sticks

Prep time: 30 minutes | Cook time: 9 minutes | Serves 4

- 455 g cod fillets
- 85 g finely ground blanched almond flour
- 2 teaspoons Old Bay seasoning
- ½ teaspoon paprika
- Sea salt and freshly ground black pepper, to taste
- 60 ml mayonnaise
- 1 large egg, beaten
- Avocado oil spray
- Tartar sauce, for serving

1. Cut the fish into ¾-inch-wide strips. 2. In a shallow bowl, stir together the almond flour, Old Bay seasoning, paprika, and salt and pepper to taste. In another shallow bowl, whisk together the mayonnaise and egg. 3. Dip the cod strips in the egg mixture, then the almond flour, gently pressing with your fingers to help adhere to the coating. 4. Place the coated fish on a baking paper-lined baking sheet and freeze for 30 minutes. 5. Spray one of the air fryer baskets with oil. Set the air fryer to 200ºC. Place the fish in the basket in a single layer, and spray each piece with oil. 6. Cook for 5 minutes. Flip and spray with more oil. Cook for 4 minutes more, until the internal temperature reaches 60ºC. Serve with the tartar sauce.

Calamari with Hot Sauce & Cornmeal-Crusted Trout Fingers

Prep time: 25 minutes | Cook time: 6 minutes | Serves 2

Calamari with Hot Sauce | Serves 2:

- 280 g calamari, trimmed
- 2 tablespoons hot sauce
- 1 tablespoon avocado oil

Cornmeal-Crusted Trout Fingers | Serves 2:

- 70 g yellow cornmeal, medium or finely ground (not coarse)
- 20 g plain flour
- 1½ teaspoons baking powder
- 1 teaspoon kosher or coarse sea salt, plus more as needed
- ½ teaspoon freshly ground black pepper, plus more as needed
- ⅛ teaspoon cayenne pepper
- 340 g skinless trout fillets, cut into strips 1 inch wide and 3 inches long
- 3 large eggs, lightly beaten
- Cooking spray
- 115 g mayonnaise
- 2 tablespoons capers, rinsed and finely chopped
- 1 tablespoon fresh tarragon
- 1 teaspoon fresh lemon juice, plus lemon wedges, for serving

Prepare for Calamari with Hot Sauce:

1. Slice the calamari and sprinkle with avocado oil.
2. Put the calamari in zone 1 drawer.

Prepare for Cornmeal-Crusted Trout Fingers:

1. Preheat the air fryer to 200ºC.
2. In a large bowl, whisk together the cornmeal, flour, baking powder, salt, black pepper, and cayenne. Dip the trout strips in the egg, then toss them in the cornmeal mixture until fully coated. Transfer the trout to a rack set over a baking sheet and liberally spray all over with cooking spray.
3. Transfer the fish to zone 2 drawer. If necessary, work in batches.
4. In a bowl, whisk together the mayonnaise, capers, tarragon, and lemon juice. Season the tartar sauce with salt and black pepper.

Cook:

1. In zone 1, set the temperature to 200ºC, set the time to 3 minutes, per side.
2. In zone 2, set the temperature to 200ºC, set the time to 6 minutes,
3. Press SYNC, then press Start.
4. Transfer the calamari in the serving plate and sprinkle with hot sauce.
5. Transfer the fish sticks to a plate and repeat with the remaining fish. Serve the trout fingers hot along with the tartar sauce and lemon wedges.

Oregano Tilapia Fingers

Prep time: 15 minutes | Cook time: 9 minutes | Serves 4

- 455 g tilapia fillet
- 30 g coconut flour
- 2 eggs, beaten
- ½ teaspoon ground paprika
- 1 teaspoon dried oregano
- 1 teaspoon avocado oil

1. Cut the tilapia fillets into fingers and sprinkle with ground paprika and dried oregano. 2. Then dip the tilapia fingers in eggs and coat in the coconut flour. 3. Sprinkle fish fingers with avocado oil and cook in the air fryer at 190ºC for 9 minutes.

Prawns with Swiss Chard

Prep time: 10 minutes | Cook time: 10 minutes | Serves 4

- 455 g prawns, peeled and deveined
- ½ teaspoon smoked paprika
- 70 g Swiss chard, chopped
- 2 tablespoons apple cider vinegar
- 1 tablespoon coconut oil
- 60 ml heavy cream

1. Mix prawns with smoked paprika and apple cider vinegar. 2. Put the prawns in zone 1 drawer and add coconut oil. 3. Cook the prawns at 180ºC for 10 minutes. 4. Then mix cooked prawns with remaining ingredients and carefully mix.

Chapter 5 Fish and Seafood | 35

Blackened Fish

Prep time: 15 minutes | Cook time: 8 minutes | Serves 4

1 large egg, beaten
Blackened seasoning, as needed
2 tablespoons light brown sugar
4 tilapia fillets, 110g each
Cooking spray

1. In a shallow bowl, place the beaten egg. In a second shallow bowl, stir together the Blackened seasoning and the brown sugar. 2. One at a time, dip the fish fillets in the egg, then the brown sugar mixture, coating thoroughly. 3. Preheat the air fryer to 150ºC. Line one of the air fryer baskets with baking paper. 4. Place the coated fish on the baking paper and spritz with oil. 5. Bake for 4 minutes. Flip the fish, spritz it with oil, and bake for 4 to 6 minutes more until the fish is white inside and flakes easily with a fork. 6. Serve immediately.

Herbed Prawns Pita

Prep time: 5 minutes | Cook time: 8 minutes | Serves 4

455 g medium prawns, peeled and deveined
2 tablespoons olive oil
1 teaspoon dried oregano
½ teaspoon dried thyme
½ teaspoon garlic powder
¼ teaspoon onion powder
½ teaspoon salt
¼ teaspoon black pepper
4 whole wheat pitas
110 g feta cheese, crumbled
75 g shredded lettuce
1 tomato, diced
45 g black olives, sliced
1 lemon

1. Preheat the oven to 190ºC. 2. In a medium bowl, combine the prawns with the olive oil, oregano, thyme, garlic powder, onion powder, salt, and black pepper. 3. Pour prawns in a single layer in zone 1 drawer and roast for 6 to 8 minutes, or until cooked through. 4. Remove from the air fryer and divide into warmed pitas with feta, lettuce, tomato, olives, and a squeeze of lemon.

Prawn Kebabs

Prep time: 15 minutes | Cook time: 6 minutes | Serves 4

Olive or vegetable oil, for spraying
455 g medium raw prawns, peeled and deveined
4 tablespoons unsalted butter, melted
1 tablespoon Old Bay seasoning
1 tablespoon packed light brown sugar
1 teaspoon granulated garlic
1 teaspoon onion powder
½ teaspoon freshly ground black pepper

1. Line one of the air fryer baskets with baking paper and spray lightly with oil. 2. Thread the prawns onto the skewers and place them in the prepared basket. 3. In a small bowl, mix together the butter, Old Bay, brown sugar, garlic, onion powder, and black pepper. Brush the sauce on the prawns. 4. Air fry at 200ºC for 5 to 6 minutes, or until pink and firm. Serve immediately.

Prawns with Smoky Tomato Dressing

Prep time: 5 minutes | Cook time: 8 minutes | Serves 2

3 tablespoons mayonnaise
1 tablespoon ketchup
1 tablespoon minced garlic
1 teaspoon Sriracha
½ teaspoon smoked paprika
½ teaspoon kosher or coarse sea salt
455 g large raw prawns (21 to 25 count), peeled (tails left on) and deveined
Vegetable oil spray
50 g chopped spring onions

1. In a large bowl, combine the mayonnaise, ketchup, garlic, Sriracha, paprika, and salt. Add the prawns and toss to coat with the sauce. 2. Spray one of the air fryer baskets with vegetable oil spray. Place the prawns in the basket. Set the air fryer to 180ºC for 8 minutes, tossing and spraying the prawns with vegetable oil spray halfway through the cooking time. 3. Sprinkle with the chopped spring onions before serving.

Cajun Catfish Cakes with Cheese

Prep time: 5 minutes | Cook time: 35 minutes | Serves 4

2 catfish fillets
85 g butter
150 g shredded Parmesan cheese
150 g shredded Swiss cheese
120 ml buttermilk
1 teaspoon baking powder
1 teaspoon baking soda
1 teaspoon Cajun seasoning

1. Bring a pot of salted water to a boil. Add the catfish fillets to the boiling water and let them boil for 5 minutes until they become opaque. 2. Remove the fillets from the pot to a mixing bowl and flake them into small pieces with a fork. 3. Add the remaining ingredients to the bowl of fish and stir until well incorporated. 4. Divide the fish mixture into 12 equal portions and shape each portion into a patty. 5. Preheat the air fryer to 190ºC. 6. Arrange the patties in one of the air fryer baskets and air fry in batches for 15 minutes until golden brown and cooked through. Flip the patties halfway through the cooking time. 7. Let the patties sit for 5 minutes and serve.

Italian Tuna Roast

Prep time: 15 minutes | Cook time: 21 to 24 minutes | Serves 8

Cooking spray
1 tablespoon Italian seasoning
⅛ teaspoon ground black pepper
1 tablespoon extra-light olive oil
1 teaspoon lemon juice
1 (900 g) tuna loin, 3 to 4 inches thick

1. Spray baking dish with cooking spray and place in 2 air fryer baskets. Preheat the air fryer to 200ºC. 2. Mix together the Italian seasoning, pepper, oil, and lemon juice. 3. Using a dull table knife or butter knife, pierce top of tuna about every half inch: Insert knife into top of tuna roast and pierce almost all the way to the bottom. 4. Spoon oil mixture into each of the holes and use the knife to push seasonings into the tuna as deeply as possible. 5. Spread any remaining oil mixture on all outer surfaces of tuna. 6. Place tuna roast in baking dish and roast for 20 minutes. Check temperature with a meat thermometer. Cook for an additional 1 to 4 minutes or until temperature reaches 64ºC. 7. Remove 2 baskets from the air fryer and let tuna sit in the baskets for 10 minutes.

Fish Gratin

Prep time: 30 minutes | Cook time: 17 minutes | Serves 4

1 tablespoon avocado oil
455 g hake fillets
1 teaspoon garlic powder
Sea salt and ground white pepper, to taste
2 tablespoons shallots, chopped
1 bell pepper, seeded and chopped
110 g cottage cheese
120 ml sour cream
1 egg, well whisked
1 teaspoon yellow mustard
1 tablespoon lime juice
60 g Swiss cheese, shredded

1. Brush the bottom and sides of a casserole dish with avocado oil. Add the hake fillets to the casserole dish and sprinkle with garlic powder, salt, and pepper. 2. Add the chopped shallots and bell peppers. 3. In a mixing bowl, thoroughly combine the Cottage cheese, sour cream, egg, mustard, and lime juice. Pour the mixture over fish and spread evenly. 4. Cook in the preheated air fryer at 190ºC for 10 minutes. 5. Top with the Swiss cheese and cook an additional 7 minutes. Let it rest for 10 minutes before slicing and serving. Bon appétit!

Lemony Salmon

Prep time: 30 minutes | Cook time: 10 minutes | Serves 4

680 g salmon steak
½ teaspoon grated lemon zest
Freshly cracked mixed peppercorns, to taste
80 ml lemon juice
Fresh chopped chives, for garnish
120 ml dry white wine, or apple cider vinegar
½ teaspoon fresh coriander, chopped
Fine sea salt, to taste

1. To prepare the marinade, place all ingredients, except for salmon steak and chives, in a deep pan. Bring to a boil over medium-high flame until it has reduced by half. Allow it to cool down. 2. After that, allow salmon steak to marinate in the refrigerator approximately 40 minutes. Discard the marinade and transfer the fish steak to the preheated air fryer. 3. Air fry at 200ºC for 9 to 10 minutes. To finish, brush hot fish steaks with the reserved marinade, garnish with fresh chopped chives, and serve right away!

Golden Beer-Battered Cod

Prep time: 5 minutes | Cook time: 15 minutes | Serves 4

2 eggs
240 ml malty beer
60 g plain flour
30 g cornflour
1 teaspoon garlic powder
Salt and pepper, to taste
4 cod fillets, 110 g each
Cooking spray

1. Preheat the air fryer to 200ºC. 2. In a shallow bowl, beat together the eggs with the beer. In another shallow bowl, thoroughly combine the flour and cornflour. Sprinkle with the garlic powder, salt, and pepper. 3. Dredge each cod fillet in the flour mixture, then in the egg mixture. Dip each piece of fish in the flour mixture a second time. 4. Spritz the air fryer basket with cooking spray. Arrange the cod fillets in 2 baskets in a single layer, half in zone 1 and the remaining in zone 2. 5. Air fry in batches for 15 minutes until the cod reaches an internal temperature of 64ºC on a meat thermometer and the outside is crispy. Flip the fillets halfway through the cooking time. 6. Let the fish cool for 5 minutes and serve.

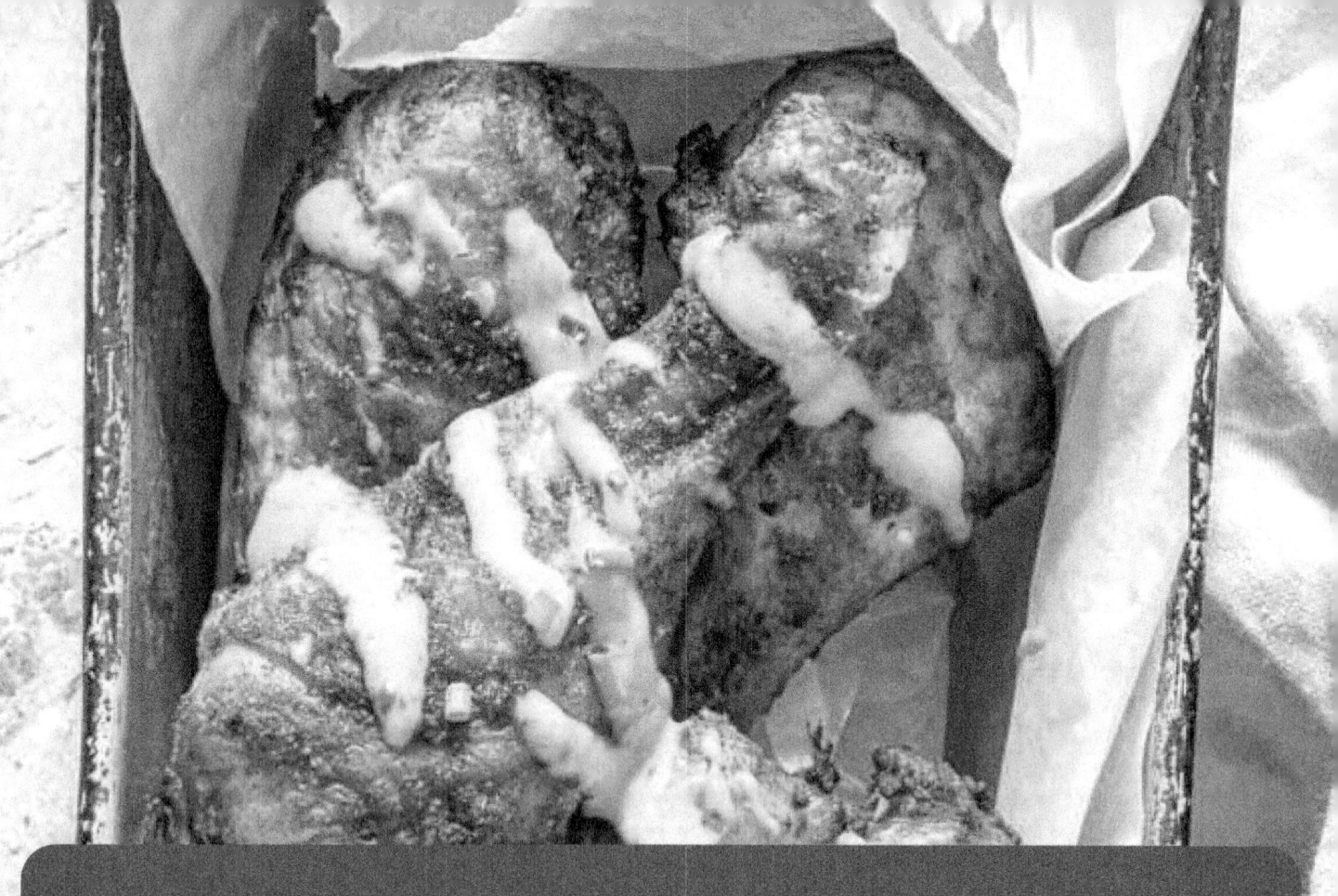

Chapter 6 Beef, Pork, and Lamb

Chapter 6 Beef, Pork, and Lamb

Chinese-Style Baby Back Ribs

Prep time: 30 minutes | Cook time: 30 minutes | Serves 4

1 tablespoon toasted sesame oil
1 tablespoon fermented black bean paste
1 tablespoon Shaoxing wine (rice cooking wine)
1 tablespoon dark soy sauce
1 tablespoon agave nectar or honey
1 teaspoon minced garlic
1 teaspoon minced fresh ginger
1 (680 g) slab baby back ribs, cut into individual ribs

1. In a large bowl, stir together the sesame oil, black bean paste, wine, soy sauce, agave, garlic, and ginger. Add the ribs and toss well to coat. Marinate at room temperature for 30 minutes, or cover and refrigerate for up to 24 hours. 2. Place the ribs in one of the air fryer baskets; discard the marinade. Set the air fryer to 180ºC for 30 minutes.

Spicy Lamb Sirloin Chops

Prep time: 30 minutes | Cook time: 15 minutes | Serves 4

½ brown onion, coarsely chopped
4 coin-size slices peeled fresh ginger
5 garlic cloves
1 teaspoon garam masala
1 teaspoon ground fennel
1 teaspoon ground cinnamon
1 teaspoon ground turmeric
½ to 1 teaspoon cayenne pepper
½ teaspoon ground cardamom
1 teaspoon coarse or flaky salt
450 g lamb sirloin chops

1. In a blender, combine the onion, ginger, garlic, garam masala, fennel, cinnamon, turmeric, cayenne, cardamom, and salt. Pulse until the onion is finely minced and the mixture forms a thick paste, 3 to 4 minutes. 2. Place the lamb chops in a large bowl. Slash the meat and fat with a sharp knife several times to allow the marinade to penetrate better. Add the spice paste to the bowl and toss the lamb to coat. Marinate at room temperature for 30 minutes or cover and refrigerate for up to 24 hours. 3. Place the lamb chops in a single layer in 2 air fryer baskets. Set the air fryer to 160ºC for 15 minutes, turning the chops halfway through the cooking time. Use a meat thermometer to ensure the lamb has reached an internal temperature of 64ºC (medium-rare).

Spicy Bavette Steak with Zhoug

Prep time: 30 minutes | Cook time: 8 minutes | Serves 4

Marinade and Steak:

120 ml dark beer or orange juice
60 g fresh lemon juice
3 cloves garlic, minced
2 tablespoons extra-virgin olive oil
2 tablespoons Sriracha
2 tablespoons brown sugar
2 teaspoons ground cumin
2 teaspoons smoked paprika
1 tablespoon coarse or flaky salt
1 teaspoon black pepper
680 g bavette or skirt steak, trimmed and cut into 3 pieces

Zhoug:

235 g packed fresh coriander leaves
2 cloves garlic, peeled
2 jalapeño or green chiles, stemmed and coarsely chopped
½ teaspoon ground cumin
¼ teaspoon ground coriander
¼ teaspoon coarse or flaky salt
2 to 4 tablespoons extra-virgin olive oil

For the marinade and steak:

1. In a small bowl, whisk together the beer, lemon juice, garlic, olive oil, Sriracha, brown sugar, cumin, paprika, salt, and pepper.
2. Place the steak in a large resealable plastic bag. Pour the marinade over the steak, seal the bag, and massage the steak to coat. Marinate in the refrigerator for 1 hour or up to 24 hours, turning the bag occasionally.
3. Remove the steak from the marinade and discard the marinade. Place half the steak in zone 1 drawer, the remaining in zone 2 drawer.

For the zhoug:

1. In a food processor, combine the coriander, garlic, jalapeños, cumin, coriander, and salt. Process until finely chopped.
2. Add 2 tablespoons olive oil and pulse to form a loose paste, adding up to 2 tablespoons more olive oil if needed.
3. Transfer the zhoug to a glass container. Cover and store in the refrigerator until 30 minutes before serving if marinating more than 1 hour.

Cook:

1. Select Zone 1, select BAKE, set the temperature to 200ºC, set the time to 8 minutes.
2. Select Zone 2, select Match Cook and press Start. Use a meat thermometer to ensure the steak has reached an internal temperature of 64ºC (for medium).
3. Transfer the steak to a cutting board and let rest for 5 minutes. Slice the steak across the grain and serve with the zhoug.

Spicy Rump Steak

Prep time: 25 minutes | Cook time: 12 to 18 minutes | Serves 4

- 2 tablespoons salsa
- 1 tablespoon minced chipotle pepper or chipotle paste
- 1 tablespoon apple cider vinegar
- 1 teaspoon ground cumin
- ⅛ teaspoon freshly ground black pepper
- ⅛ teaspoon red pepper flakes
- 340 g rump steak, cut into 4 pieces and gently pounded to about ⅓ inch thick
- Cooking oil spray

1. In a small bowl, thoroughly mix the salsa, chipotle pepper, vinegar, cumin, black pepper, and red pepper flakes. Rub this mixture into both sides of each steak piece. Let stand for 15 minutes at room temperature. 2. Insert the crisper plate into the basket and place the basket into the unit. Preheat the unit by selecting AIR FRY, setting the temperature to 200°C, and setting the time to 3 minutes. Select START/STOP to begin. 3. Once the unit is preheated, spray the crisper plate with cooking oil. Working in batches, place one steak in zone 1, the remaining in zone 2. 4. In zone 1, Select AIR FRY, set the temperature to 200°C, and set the time to 9 minutes. In zone 2, select Match Cook and press Start. 5. After about 6 minutes, check the steaks. If a food thermometer inserted into the meat registers at least 64°C, they are done. If not, resume cooking. 6. When the cooking is done, transfer the steaks to a clean plate and cover with aluminum foil to keep warm. Repeat steps 3, 4, and 5 with the remaining steaks. 7. Thinly slice the steaks against the grain and serve.

Fruited Ham

Prep time: 15 minutes | Cook time: 8 to 10 minutes | Serves 4

- 235 ml orange marmalade
- 48 g packed light brown sugar
- ¼ teaspoon ground cloves
- ½ teaspoon mustard powder
- 1 to 2 tablespoons oil
- 450 g cooked ham, cut into 1-inch cubes
- 120 g canned mandarin oranges, drained and chopped

1. In a small bowl, stir together the orange marmalade, brown sugar, cloves, and mustard powder until blended. Set aside. 2. Preheat the air fryer to 160°C. Spritz a baking tray with oil. 3. Place the ham cubes in the prepared pan. Pour the marmalade sauce over the ham to glaze it. 4. Cook for 4 minutes. Stir and cook for 2 minutes more. 5. Add the mandarin oranges and cook for 2 to 4 minutes more until the sauce begins to thicken and the ham is tender.

Italian Sausages with Peppers and Onions

Prep time: 5 minutes | Cook time: 28 minutes | Serves 3

- 1 medium onion, thinly sliced
- 1 yellow or orange pepper, thinly sliced
- 1 red pepper, thinly sliced
- 60 ml avocado oil or melted coconut oil
- 1 teaspoon fine sea salt
- 6 Italian-seasoned sausages
- Dijon mustard, for serving (optional)

1. Preheat the air fryer to 200°C. 2. Place the onion and peppers in a large bowl. Drizzle with the oil and toss well to coat the veggies. Season with the salt. 3. Place the onion and peppers in a pie pan and cook in the air fryer for 8 minutes, stirring halfway through. Remove from the air fryer and set aside. 4. Spray one of the air fryer baskets with avocado oil. Place the sausages in the air fryer basket and air fry for 20 minutes, or until crispy and golden brown. During the last minute or two of cooking, add the onion and peppers to the basket with the sausages to warm them through. 5. Place the onion and peppers on a serving platter and arrange the sausages on top. Serve Dijon mustard on the side, if desired. 6. Store leftovers in an airtight container in the fridge for up to 7 days or in the freezer for up to a month. Reheat in a preheated 200°C air fryer for 3 minutes, or until heated through.

Fillet with Crispy Shallots

Prep time: 30 minutes | Cook time: 18 to 20 minutes | Serves 6

- 680 g beef fillet steaks
- Sea salt and freshly ground black pepper, to taste
- 4 medium shallots
- 1 teaspoon olive oil or avocado oil

1. Season both sides of the steaks with salt and pepper, and let them sit at room temperature for 45 minutes. 2. Set the air fryer to 200°C and let it preheat for 5 minutes. 3. Working in batches if necessary, place the steaks half in zone 1, the remaining in zone 2 in a single layer and air fry for 5 minutes. Flip and cook for 5 minutes longer, until an instant-read thermometer inserted in the center of the steaks registers 49°C for medium-rare (or as desired). Remove the steaks and tent with aluminum foil to rest. 4. Set the air fryer to 150°C. In a medium bowl, toss the shallots with the oil. Place the shallots in the basket and air fry for 5 minutes, then give them a toss and cook for 3 to 5 minutes more, until crispy and golden brown. 5. Place the steaks on serving plates and arrange the shallots on top.

Spice-Rubbed Pork Loin

Prep time: 5 minutes | Cook time: 20 minutes | Serves 6

- 1 teaspoon paprika
- ½ teaspoon ground cumin
- ½ teaspoon chili powder
- ½ teaspoon garlic powder
- 2 tablespoons coconut oil
- 1 (680 g) boneless pork loin
- ½ teaspoon salt
- ¼ teaspoon ground black pepper

1. In a small bowl, mix paprika, cumin, chili powder, and garlic powder. 2. Drizzle coconut oil over pork. Sprinkle pork loin with salt and pepper, then rub spice mixture evenly on all sides. 3. Place pork loin into ungreased air fryer baskets, half in zone 1, the remaining in zone 2. Adjust the temperature to 210ºC and air fry for 20 minutes, turning pork halfway through cooking. Pork loin will be browned and have an internal temperature of at least 64ºC when done. Serve warm.

Mozzarella Stuffed Beef and Pork Meatballs

Prep time: 15 minutes | Cook time: 12 minutes | Serves 4 to 6

- 1 tablespoon olive oil
- 1 small onion, finely chopped
- 1 to 2 cloves garlic, minced
- 340 g beef mince
- 340 g pork mince
- 90 g bread crumbs
- 60 g grated Parmesan cheese
- 60 g finely chopped fresh parsley
- ½ teaspoon dried oregano
- 1½ teaspoons salt
- Freshly ground black pepper, to taste
- 2 eggs, lightly beaten
- 140 g low-moisture Mozzarella or other melting cheese, cut into 1-inch cubes

1. Preheat a skillet over medium-high heat. Add the oil and cook the onion and garlic until tender, but not browned. 2. Transfer the onion and garlic to a large bowl and add the beef, pork, bread crumbs, Parmesan cheese, parsley, oregano, salt, pepper and eggs. Mix well until all the ingredients are combined. Divide the mixture into 12 evenly sized balls. Make one meatball at a time, by pressing a hole in the meatball mixture with the finger and pushing a piece of Mozzarella cheese into the hole. Mold the meat back into a ball, enclosing the cheese. 3. Preheat the air fryer to 190ºC. 4. Put half the meatballs in zone 1, the remaining in zone 2. In zone 1, select Air Fry button, adjust temperature to 190ºC, set time to 12 minutes. In zone 2, select Match Cook and press Start. If necessary, work in batches. Repeat with the remaining meatballs. Serve warm.

Sesame Beef Lettuce Tacos

Prep time: 30 minutes | Cook time: 8 to 10 minutes | Serves 4

- 60 ml soy sauce or tamari
- 60 ml avocado oil
- 2 tablespoons cooking sherry
- 1 tablespoon granulated sweetener
- 1 tablespoon ground cumin
- 1 teaspoon minced garlic
- Sea salt and freshly ground black pepper, to taste
- 450 g bavette or skirt steak
- 8 butterhead lettuce leaves
- 2 spring onions, sliced
- 1 tablespoon toasted sesame seeds
- Hot sauce, for serving
- Lime wedges, for serving
- Flaky sea salt (optional)

1. In a small bowl, whisk together the soy sauce, avocado oil, cooking sherry, sweetener, cumin, garlic, and salt and pepper to taste. 2. Place the steak in a shallow dish. Pour the marinade over the beef. Cover the dish with plastic wrap and let it marinate in the refrigerator for at least 2 hours or overnight. 3. Remove the flank steak from the dish and discard the marinade. 4. Set the air fryer to 200ºC. Place the steak in the air fryer baskets and air fry for 4 to 6 minutes. Flip the steak and cook for 4 minutes more, until an instant-read thermometer reads 49ºC at the thickest part (or cook it to your desired doneness). Allow the steak to rest for 10 minutes, then slice it thinly against the grain. 5. Stack 2 lettuce leaves on top of each other and add some sliced meat. Top with spring onions and sesame seeds. Drizzle with hot sauce and lime juice, and finish with a little flaky salt (if using). Repeat with the remaining lettuce leaves and fillings.

Peppercorn-Crusted Beef Fillet

Prep time: 10 minutes | Cook time: 25 minutes | Serves 6

- 2 tablespoons salted melted butter
- 2 teaspoons minced roasted garlic
- 3 tablespoons ground 4-peppercorn blend
- 1 (900 g) beef fillet, trimmed of visible fat

1. In a small bowl, mix the butter and roasted garlic. Brush it over the beef fillet. 2. Place the ground peppercorns onto a plate and roll the fillet through them, creating a crust. Place fillet half in zone 1, the remaining in zone 2. 3. Adjust the temperature to 200ºC and roast for 25 minutes. 4. Turn the fillet halfway through the cooking time. 5. Allow meat to rest 10 minutes before slicing.

Kielbasa Sausage with Pineapple and Peppers

Prep time: 15 minutes | Cook time: 10 minutes | Serves 2 to 4

340 g kielbasa sausage, cut into ½-inch slices
1 (230 g) can pineapple chunks in juice, drained
235 g pepper chunks
1 tablespoon barbecue seasoning
1 tablespoon soy sauce
Cooking spray

1. Preheat the air fryer to 200°C. Spritz the air fryer basket with cooking spray. 2. Combine all the ingredients in a large bowl. Toss to mix well. 3. Pour the sausage mixture in the preheated air fryer. 4. Air fry for 10 minutes or until the sausage is lightly browned and the pepper and pineapple are soft. Shake the basket halfway through. Serve immediately.

Steak, Broccoli, and Mushroom Rice Bowls

Prep time: 10 minutes | Cook time: 15 to 18 minutes | Serves 4

2 tablespoons cornflour
120 ml low-sodium beef stock
1 teaspoon reduced-salt soy sauce
340 g rump steak, cut into 1-inch cubes
120 g broccoli florets
1 onion, chopped
235 g sliced white or chestnut mushrooms
1 tablespoon grated peeled fresh ginger
Cooked brown rice (optional), for serving

1. In a medium bowl, stir together the cornflour, beef stock, and soy sauce until the cornflour is completely dissolved. 2. Add the beef cubes and toss to coat. Let stand for 5 minutes at room temperature. 3. Insert the crisper plate into the basket and the basket into the unit. Preheat the unit by selecting AIR FRY, setting the temperature to 200°C, and setting the time to 3 minutes. Select START/STOP to begin. 4. Once the unit is preheated, use a slotted spoon to transfer the beef from the stock mixture into a medium metal bowl that fits into one of the baskets. Reserve the stock. Add the broccoli, onion, mushrooms, and ginger to the beef. Place the bowl into the basket. 5. Select AIR FRY, set the temperature to 200°C, and set the time to 18 minutes. Select START/STOP to begin. 6. After about 12 minutes, check the beef and broccoli. If a food thermometer inserted into the beef registers at least 64°C and the vegetables are tender, add the reserved stock and resume cooking for about 3 minutes until the sauce boils. If not, resume cooking for about 3 minutes before adding the reservedstock. 7. When the cooking is complete, serve immediately over hot cooked brown rice, if desired.

Steak with Bell Pepper

Prep time: 30 minutes | Cook time: 20 to 23 minutes | Serves 6

60 ml avocado oil
60 g freshly squeezed lime juice
2 teaspoons minced garlic
1 tablespoon chili powder
½ teaspoon ground cumin
Sea salt and freshly ground black pepper, to taste
450 g top rump steak or bavette or skirt steak, thinly sliced against the grain
1 red pepper, cored, seeded, and cut into ½-inch slices
1 green pepper, cored, seeded, and cut into ½-inch slices
1 large onion, sliced

1. In a small bowl or blender, combine the avocado oil, lime juice, garlic, chili powder, cumin, and salt and pepper to taste. 2. Place the sliced steak in a zip-top bag or shallow dish. Place the peppers and onion in a separate zip-top bag or dish. Pour half the marinade over the steak and the other half over the vegetables. Seal both bags and let the steak and vegetables marinate in the refrigerator for at least 1 hour or up to 4 hours. 3. Line the air fryer basket with an air fryer liner or aluminum foil. Remove the vegetables from their bag or dish and shake off any excess marinade. Set the air fryer to 200°C. Place the vegetables half in zone 1, the remaining in zone 2, and cook for 13 minutes. 4. Remove the steak from its bag or dish and shake off any excess marinade. Place the steak on top of the vegetables in the air fryer, and cook for 7 to 10 minutes or until an instant-read thermometer reads 49°C for medium-rare (or cook to your desired doneness). 5. Serve with desired fixings, such as keto tortillas, lettuce, sour cream, avocado slices, shredded Cheddar cheese, and coriander.

Air Fryer Chicken-Fried Steak

Prep time: 5 minutes | Cook time: 20 minutes | Serves 4

450 g beef braising steak
700 ml low-fat milk, divided
1 teaspoon dried thyme
1 teaspoon dried rosemary
2 medium egg whites
120 g gluten-free breadcrumbs
60 g coconut flour
1 tablespoon Cajun seasoning

1. In a bowl, marinate the steak in 475 ml of milk for 30 to 45 minutes. 2. Remove the steak from milk, shake off the excess liquid, and season with the thyme and rosemary. Discard the milk. 3. In a shallow bowl, beat the egg whites with the remaining 235 ml of milk. 4. In a separate shallow bowl, combine the breadcrumbs, coconut flour, and seasoning. 5. Dip the steak in the egg white mixture then dredge in the breadcrumb mixture, coating well. 6. Place the steak in one of the baskets of the fryer. 7. Set the air fryer to 200°C, close, and cook for 10 minutes. 8. Open the air fryer, turn the steaks, close, and cook for 10 minutes. Let rest for 5 minutes.

Bacon-Wrapped Hot Dogs with Mayo-Ketchup Sauce

Prep time: 5 minutes | Cook time: 10 to 12 minutes | Serves 5

10 thin slices of bacon	60 ml mayonnaise
5 pork hot dogs, halved	4 tablespoons ketchup
1 teaspoon cayenne pepper	1 teaspoon rice vinegar
Sauce:	1 teaspoon chili powder

1. Preheat the air fryer to 200ºC. 2. Arrange the slices of bacon on a clean work surface. One by one, place the halved hot dog on one end of each slice, season with cayenne pepper and wrap the hot dog with the bacon slices and secure with toothpicks as needed. 3. Work in batches, place half the wrapped hot dogs in zone 1, the remaining in zone 2 and air fry for 10 to 12 minutes or until the bacon becomes browned and crispy. 4. Make the sauce: Stir all the ingredients for the sauce in a small bowl. Wrap the bowl in plastic and set in the refrigerator until ready to serve. 5. Transfer the hot dogs to a platter and serve hot with the sauce.

Lamb Burger with Feta and Olives

Prep time: 10 minutes | Cook time: 20 minutes | Serves 3 to 4

2 teaspoons olive oil	120 g black olives, finely chopped
⅓ onion, finely chopped	80 g crumbled feta cheese
1 clove garlic, minced	½ teaspoon salt
450 g lamb mince	Freshly ground black pepper, to taste
2 tablespoons fresh parsley, finely chopped	4 thick pitta breads
1½ teaspoons fresh oregano, finely chopped	

1. Preheat a medium skillet over medium-high heat on the stovetop. Add the olive oil and cook the onion until tender, but not browned, about 4 to 5 minutes. Add the garlic and cook for another minute. Transfer the onion and garlic to a mixing bowl and add the lamb mince, parsley, oregano, olives, feta cheese, salt and pepper. Gently mix the ingredients together. 2. Divide the mixture into 3 or 4 equal portions and then form the hamburgers, being careful not to over-handle the meat. One good way to do this is to throw the meat back and forth between your hands like a baseball, packing the meat each time you catch it. Flatten the balls into patties, making an indentation in the center of each patty. Flatten the sides of the patties as well to make it easier to fit them into the air fryer basket. 3. Preheat the air fryer to 190ºC. 4. If you don't have room for all four burgers, air fry two or three burgers at a time for 8 minutes at 190ºC. Flip the burgers over and air fry for another 8 minutes. If you cooked your burgers in batches, return the first batch of burgers to the air fryer for the last two minutes of cooking to re-heat. This should give you a medium-well burger. If you'd prefer a medium-rare burger, shorten the cooking time to about 13 minutes. Remove the burgers to a resting plate and let the burgers rest for a few minutes before dressing and serving. 5. While the burgers are resting, toast the pitta breads in the air fryer for 2 minutes. Tuck the burgers into the toasted pitta breads, or wrap the pittas around the burgers and serve with a tzatziki sauce or some mayonnaise.

Beef Burger

Prep time: 20 minutes | Cook time: 12 minutes | Serves 4

570 g lean beef mince	½ teaspoon cumin powder
1 tablespoon soy sauce or tamari	60 g spring onions, minced
	⅓ teaspoon sea salt flakes
1 teaspoon Dijon mustard	⅓ teaspoon freshly cracked mixed peppercorns
1/2 teaspoon smoked paprika	
1 teaspoon shallot powder	1 teaspoon celery salt
1 clove garlic, minced	1 teaspoon dried parsley

1. Mix all of the above ingredients in a bowl; knead until everything is well incorporated. 2. Shape the mixture into four patties. Next, make a shallow dip in the center of each patty to prevent them puffing up during air frying. 3. Spritz the patties on all sides using nonstick cooking spray. Cook approximately 12 minutes at 180ºC. 4. Check for doneness, an instant-read thermometer should read 72ºC. Bon appétit!

Herb-Roasted Beef Tips with Onions

Prep time: 5 minutes | Cook time: 10 minutes | Serves 4

450 g rib eye steak, cubed	1 teaspoon salt
2 garlic cloves, minced	½ teaspoon black pepper
2 tablespoons olive oil	1 brown onion, thinly sliced
1 tablespoon fresh oregano	

1. Preheat the air fryer to 190ºC. 2. In a medium bowl, combine the steak, garlic, olive oil, oregano, salt, pepper, and onion. Mix until all of the beef and onion are well coated. 3. Put the seasoned steak mixture into one of the air fryer baskets. Roast for 5 minutes. Stir and roast for 5 minutes more. 4. Let rest for 5 minutes before serving with some favourite sides.

Teriyaki Rump Steak with Broccoli and Capsicum

Prep time: 5 minutes | Cook time: 13 minutes | Serves 4

230 g rump steak	2 red peppers, sliced
80 ml teriyaki marinade	Fine sea salt and ground black pepper, to taste
1½ teaspoons sesame oil	
½ head broccoli, cut into florets	Cooking spray

1. Toss the rump steak in a large bowl with teriyaki marinade. Wrap the bowl in plastic and refrigerate to marinate for at least an hour. 2. Preheat the air fryer to 200°C and spritz with cooking spray. 3. Discard the marinade and transfer the steak in the preheated air fryer. Spritz with cooking spray. 4. Air fry for 13 minutes or until well browned. Flip the steak halfway through. 5. Meanwhile, heat the sesame oil in a nonstick skillet over medium heat. Add the broccoli and red pepper. Sprinkle with salt and ground black pepper. Sauté for 5 minutes or until the broccoli is tender. 6. Transfer the air fried rump steak on a plate and top with the sautéed broccoli and pepper. Serve hot.

Minute Steak Roll-Ups

Prep time: 30 minutes | Cook time: 8 to 10 minutes | Serves 4

4 minute steaks (170 g each)	onion
1 (450 g) bottle Italian dressing	120 g finely chopped green pepper
1 teaspoon salt	120 g finely chopped mushrooms
½ teaspoon freshly ground black pepper	
120 g finely chopped brown	1 to 2 tablespoons oil

1. In a large resealable bag or airtight storage container, combine the steaks and Italian dressing. Seal the bag and refrigerate to marinate for 2 hours. 2. Remove the steaks from the marinade and place them on a cutting board. Discard the marinade. Evenly season the steaks with salt and pepper. 3. In a small bowl, stir together the onion, pepper, and mushrooms. Sprinkle the onion mixture evenly over the steaks. Roll up the steaks, jelly roll-style, and secure with toothpicks. 4. Preheat the air fryer to 200°C. 5. Place the steaks in the air fryer baskets. 6. Cook for 4 minutes. Flip the steaks and spritz them with oil. Cook for 4 to 6 minutes more until the internal temperature reaches 64°C. Let rest for 5 minutes before serving.

Fajita Meatball Lettuce Wraps

Prep time: 10 minutes | Cook time: 10 minutes | Serves 4

450 g beef mince (85% lean)	½ teaspoon chili powder
120 ml salsa, plus more for serving if desired	½ teaspoon ground cumin
	1 clove garlic, minced
60 g chopped onions	For Serving (Optional):
60 g diced green or red peppers	8 leaves butterhead lettuce
1 large egg, beaten	Pico de gallo or salsa
1 teaspoon fine sea salt	Lime slices

1. Spray one of the air fryer baskets with avocado oil. Preheat the air fryer to 180°C. 2. In a large bowl, mix together all the ingredients until well combined. 3. Shape the meat mixture into eight 1-inch balls. Place the meatballs in the air fryer basket, leaving a little space between them. Air fry for 10 minutes, or until cooked through and no longer pink inside and the internal temperature reaches 64°C. 4. Serve each meatball on a lettuce leaf, topped with pico de gallo or salsa, if desired. Serve with lime slices if desired. 5. Store leftovers in an airtight container in the fridge for 3 days or in the freezer for up to a month. Reheat in a preheated 180°C air fryer for 4 minutes, or until heated through.

Marinated Steak Tips with Mushrooms

Prep time: 30 minutes | Cook time: 10 minutes | Serves 4

680 g rump steak, trimmed and cut into 1-inch pieces	1 tablespoon olive oil
	1 teaspoon paprika
230 g brown mushrooms, halved	1 teaspoon crushed red pepper flakes
60 ml Worcestershire sauce	2 tablespoons chopped fresh parsley (optional)
1 tablespoon Dijon mustard	

1. Place the beef and mushrooms in a gallon-size resealable bag. In a small bowl, whisk together the Worcestershire, mustard, olive oil, paprika, and red pepper flakes. Pour the marinade into the bag and massage gently to ensure the beef and mushrooms are evenly coated. Seal the bag and refrigerate for at least 4 hours, preferably overnight. Remove from the refrigerator 30 minutes before cooking. 2. Preheat the air fryer to 200°C. 3. Drain and discard the marinade. Arrange the steak and mushrooms in one of the air fryer baskets. Air fry for 10 minutes, pausing halfway through the baking time to shake the basket. Transfer to a serving plate and top with the parsley, if desired.

Vietnamese "Shaking" Beef

Prep time: 30 minutes | Cook time: 4 minutes per batch | Serves 4

Meat:

4 garlic cloves, minced
2 teaspoons soy sauce
2 teaspoons sugar
1 teaspoon toasted sesame oil
1 teaspoon coarse or flaky salt
¼ teaspoon black pepper
680 g flat iron or top rump steak, cut into 1-inch cubes

Salad:

2 tablespoons rice vinegar or apple cider vinegar
2 tablespoons vegetable oil
1 garlic clove, minced
2 teaspoons sugar
¼ teaspoon coarse or flaky salt
¼ teaspoon black pepper
½ red onion, halved and very thinly sliced
1 head butterhead lettuce, leaves separated and torn into large pieces
120 g halved baby plum tomatoes
60 g fresh mint leaves
For Serving:
Lime wedges
Coarse salt and freshly cracked black pepper, to taste

1. For the meat: In a small bowl, combine the garlic, soy sauce, sugar, sesame oil, salt, and pepper. Place the meat in a gallon-size resealable plastic bag. Pour the marinade over the meat. Seal and place the bag in a large bowl. Marinate for 30 minutes, or cover and refrigerate for up to 24 hours. 2. Place half the meat in the air fryer basket. Set the air fryer to 230°C for 4 minutes, shaking the basket to redistribute the meat halfway through the cooking time. Transfer the meat to a plate (it should be medium-rare, still pink in the middle). Cover lightly with aluminum foil. Repeat to cook the remaining meat. 3. Meanwhile, for the salad: In a large bowl, whisk together the vinegar, vegetable oil, garlic, sugar, salt, and pepper. Add the onion. Stir to combine. Add the lettuce, tomatoes, and mint and toss to combine. Arrange the salad on a serving platter. 4. Arrange the cooked meat over the salad. Drizzle any accumulated juices from the plate over the meat. Serve with lime wedges, coarse salt, and cracked black pepper.

Greek-Style Meatloaf

Prep time: 5 minutes | Cook time: 25 minutes | Serves 6

450 g lean beef mince
2 eggs
2 plum tomatoes, diced
½ brown onion, diced
60 g whole wheat bread crumbs
1 teaspoon garlic powder
1 teaspoon dried oregano
1 teaspoon dried thyme
1 teaspoon salt
1 teaspoon black pepper
60 g mozzarella cheese, shredded
1 tablespoon olive oil
Fresh chopped parsley, for garnish

1. Preheat the oven to 190°C. 2. In a large bowl, mix together the beef, eggs, tomatoes, onion, bread crumbs, garlic powder, oregano, thyme, salt, pepper, and cheese. 3. Form into a loaf, flattening to 1-inch thick. 4. Brush the top with olive oil, then place the meatloaf half in zone 1, the remaining in zone 2, and cook for 25 minutes. 5. Remove from the air fryer and allow to rest for 5 minutes, before slicing and serving with a sprinkle of parsley.

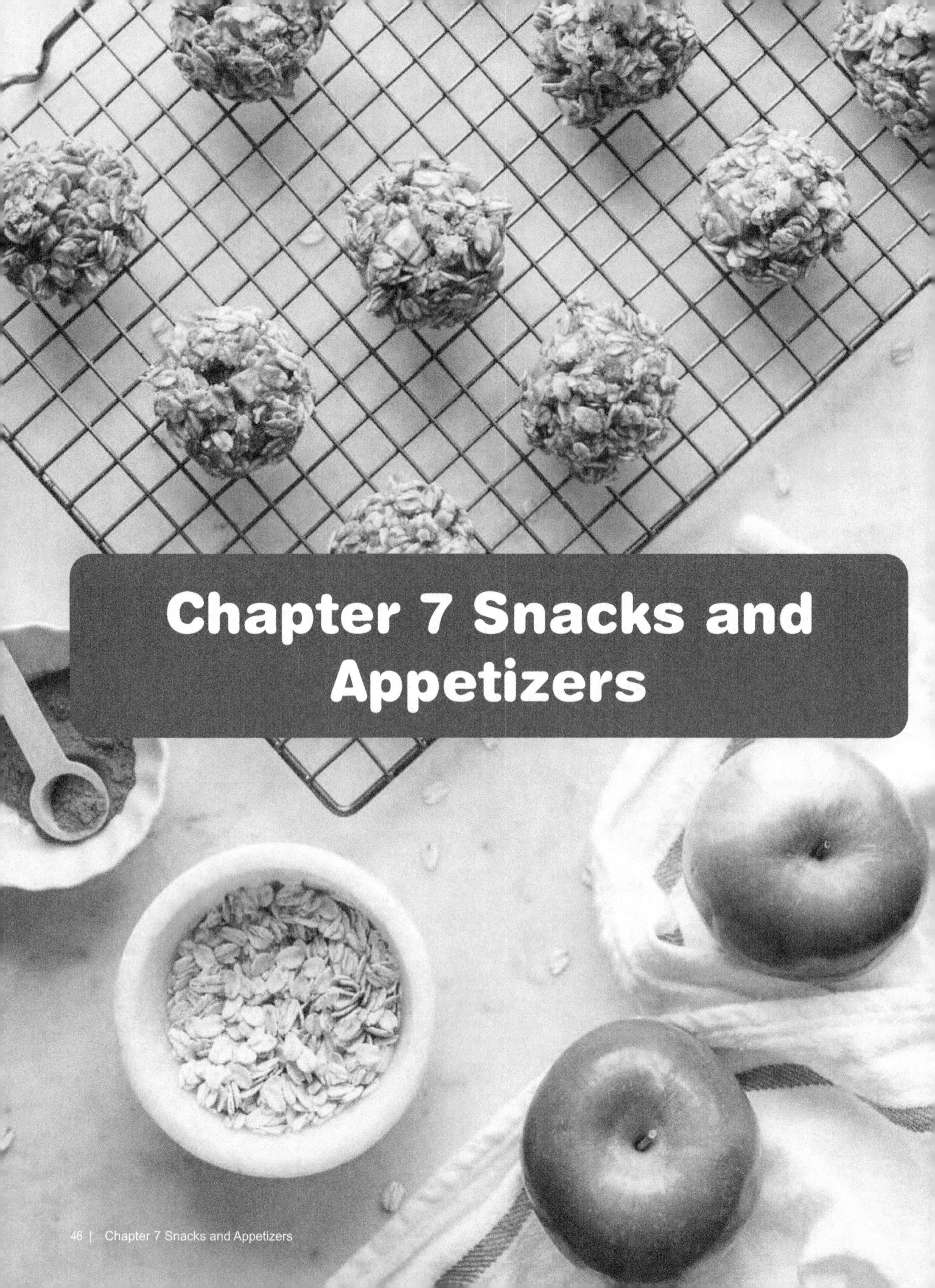

Chapter 7 Snacks and Appetizers

Chapter 7 Snacks and Appetizers

Browned Ricotta with Capers and Lemon

Prep time: 10 minutes | Cook time: 8 to 10 minutes | Serves 4 to 6

320 g whole milk ricotta cheese
2 tablespoons extra-virgin olive oil
2 tablespoons capers, rinsed
Zest of 1 lemon, plus more for garnish
1 teaspoon finely chopped fresh rosemary
Pinch crushed red pepper flakes
Salt and freshly ground black pepper, to taste
1 tablespoon grated Parmesan cheese

1. Preheat the air fryer to 190°C. 2. In a mixing bowl, stir together the ricotta cheese, olive oil, capers, lemon zest, rosemary, red pepper flakes, salt, and pepper until well combined. 3. Spread the mixture evenly in a baking dish and place it in zone 1 drawer. 4. Air fry for 8 to 10 minutes until the top is nicely browned. 5. Remove from the basket and top with a sprinkle of grated Parmesan cheese. 6. Garnish with the lemon zest and serve warm.

Rumaki

Prep time: 30 minutes | Cook time: 10 to 12 minutes per batch | Makes about 24 rumaki

283 g raw chicken livers
1 can sliced water chestnuts, drained
60 ml low-salt teriyaki sauce
12 slices turkey bacon

1. Cut livers into 1½-inch pieces, trimming out tough veins as you slice. 2. Place livers, water chestnuts, and teriyaki sauce in small container with lid. If needed, add another tablespoon of teriyaki sauce to make sure livers are covered. Refrigerate for 1 hour. 3. When ready to cook, cut bacon slices in half crosswise. 4. Wrap 1 piece of liver and 1 slice of water chestnut in each bacon strip. Secure with a cocktail stick. 5. When you have wrapped half of the livers, place them in both zone 1 drawer and zone 2 drawer in a single layer. 6. Air fry at 200°C for 10 to 12 minutes, until liver is done, and bacon is crispy. 7. While first batch cooks, wrap the remaining livers. Repeat step 6 to cook your second batch.

Crunchy Basil White Beans

Prep time: 2 minutes | Cook time: 19 minutes | Serves 2

1 (425 g) can cooked white beans
2 tablespoons olive oil
1 teaspoon fresh sage, chopped
¼ teaspoon garlic powder
¼ teaspoon salt, divided
1 teaspoon chopped fresh basil

1. Preheat the air fryer to 190°C. 2. In a medium-sized bowl, mix together the beans, olive oil, sage, garlic, ⅛ teaspoon salt, and basil. 3. Pour the white beans into zone 1 drawer and spread them out in a single layer. 4. Bake for 10 minutes. Stir and continue cooking for an additional 5 to 9 minutes, or until they reach your preferred level of crispiness. 5. Toss with the remaining ⅛ teaspoon salt before serving.

Sausage Balls with Cheese

Prep time: 10 minutes | Cook time: 10 to 11 minutes | Serves 8

340 g mild sausage meat
177 g baking mix
120 g shredded mild Cheddar cheese
85 g soft white cheese, at room temperature
1 to 2 tablespoons olive oil

1. Preheat the air fryer to 160°C. Line the air fryer basket with baking paper paper. 2. Mix together the ground sausage, baking mix, Cheddar cheese, and soft white cheese in a large bowl and stir to incorporate. 3. Divide the sausage mixture into 16 equal portions and roll them into 1-inch balls with your hands. 4. Arrange the sausage balls on the baking paper, then put them half in zone 1 and the remaining in zone 2, leaving space between each ball, then put them half in zone 1 and the remaining in zone 2. You may need to work in batches to avoid overcrowding. 5. Brush the sausage balls with the olive oil. Bake for 10 to 11 minutes, shaking the basket halfway through, or until the balls are firm and lightly browned on both sides. 6. Remove from the basket to a plate and repeat with the remaining balls. 7. Serve warm.

Pickle Chips

Prep time: 30 minutes | Cook time: 12 minutes | Serves 4

Oil, for spraying
40 g sliced fresh dill or 240 g sweet gherkins, drained
240 ml buttermilk
245 g plain flour
2 large eggs, beaten
110 g panko breadcrumbs
¼ teaspoon salt

1. Line the air fryer basket with baking paper and spray lightly with oil. 2. In a shallow dish, combine the pickled cucumbers and buttermilk and let soak for at least 1 hour, then drain. 3. Place the flour, beaten eggs, and breadcrumbs in separate bowls. 4. Coat each pickle chip lightly in the flour, dip in the eggs, and dredge in the breadcrumbs. Be sure each one is evenly coated. 5. Place the pickle chips in the prepared basket, sprinkle with the salt, and spray lightly with oil. You may need to work in batches, depending on the size of your air fryer. 6. Air fry at 200ºC for 5 minutes, flip, and cook for another 5 to 7 minutes, or until crispy. Serve hot.

Authentic Scotch Eggs

Prep time: 15 minutes | Cook time: 11 to 13 minutes | Serves 6

680 g bulk lean chicken or turkey sausage
3 raw eggs, divided
100 g dried breadcrumbs, divided
65 g plain flour
6 hardboiled eggs, peeled
Cooking oil spray

1. In a large bowl, combine the chicken sausage, 1 raw egg, and 40 g of breadcrumbs and mix well. Divide the mixture into 6 pieces and flatten each into a long oval. 2. In a shallow dish, beat the remaining 2 raw eggs. 3. Place the flour in a small bowl. 4. Place the remaining 80 g of breadcrumbs in a second small bowl. 5. Roll each hardboiled egg in the flour and wrap one of the chicken sausage pieces around each egg to encircle it completely. 6. One at a time, roll the encased eggs in the flour, dip in the beaten eggs, and finally dip in the breadcrumbs to coat. 7. Insert the crisper plate into the basket and the basket into the unit. Preheat the unit by selecting AIR FRY, setting the temperature to 190ºC, and setting the time to 3 minutes. Select START/STOP to begin. 8. Once the unit is preheated, spray the crisper plate with cooking oil. Place the eggs in a single layer half in zone 1, the remaining in zone 2, and spray them with oil. 9. In zone 1, select Air fry button, adjust temperature to 190ºC, set time to 13 minutes. In zone 2, select Match Cook and press Start. 10. After about 6 minutes, use tongs to turn the eggs and spray them with more oil. Resume cooking for 5 to 7 minutes more, or until the chicken is thoroughly cooked and the Scotch eggs are browned. 11. When the cooking is complete, serve warm.

Roasted Pearl Onion Dip

Prep time: 5 minutes | Cook time: 12 minutes | Serves 4

275 g peeled pearl onions
3 garlic cloves
3 tablespoons olive oil, divided
½ teaspoon salt
240 ml non-fat plain Greek yoghurt
1 tablespoon lemon juice
¼ teaspoon black pepper
⅛ teaspoon red pepper flakes
Pitta chips, mixed vegetables, or toasted bread for serving (optional)

1. Preheat the air fryer to 180ºC. 2. In a large bowl, combine the pearl onions and garlic with 2 tablespoons of the olive oil until the onions are well coated. 3. Pour the garlic-and-onion mixture into one of the air fryer baskets and roast for 12 minutes. 4. Transfer the garlic and onions to a food processor. Pulse the mixed vegetables several times, until the onions are minced but still have some chunks. 5. In a large bowl, combine the garlic and onions and the remaining 1 tablespoon of olive oil, along with the salt, yoghurt, lemon juice, black pepper, and red pepper flakes. 6. Cover and chill for 1 hour before serving with pitta chips, mixed vegetables, or toasted bread.

Crispy Green Bean Fries with Lemon-Yoghurt Sauce

Prep time: 5 minutes | Cook time: 5 minutes | Serves 4

French beans:

1 egg
2 tablespoons water
1 tablespoon wholemeal flour
¼ teaspoon paprika
½ teaspoon garlic powder
½ teaspoon salt
25 g wholemeal breadcrumbs
227 g whole French beans

Lemon-Yoghurt Sauce:

120 ml non-fat plain Greek yoghurt
1 tablespoon lemon juice
¼ teaspoon salt
⅛ teaspoon cayenne pepper

Make the French beans: 1. Preheat the air fryer to 190ºC. 2. In a medium shallow dish, beat together the egg and water until frothy. 3. In a separate medium shallow dish, whisk together the flour, paprika, garlic powder, and salt, then mix in the breadcrumbs. 4. Spray the bottom of the air fryer with cooking spray. 5. Dip each green bean into the egg mixture, then into the bread crumb mixture, coating the outside with the crumbs. Place the French beans in a single layer in the bottom of one of the air fryer baskets. 6. Fry in the air fryer for 5 minutes, or until the breading is golden. Make the Lemon-Yoghurt Sauce: 7. In a small bowl, combine the yoghurt, lemon juice, salt, and cayenne. 8. Serve the green bean fries alongside the lemon-yoghurt sauce as a snack or appetizer.

Garlic-Roasted Tomatoes and Olives

Prep time: 5 minutes | Cook time: 20 minutes | Serves 6

300 g cherry tomatoes
4 garlic cloves, roughly chopped
½ red onion, roughly chopped
160 g black olives
180 g green olives
1 tablespoon fresh basil, minced
1 tablespoon fresh oregano, minced
2 tablespoons olive oil
¼ to ½ teaspoon salt

1. Preheat the air fryer to 190ºC. 2. In a large bowl, combine all of the ingredients and toss together so that the tomatoes and olives are coated well with the olive oil and herbs. 3. Pour the mixture into 2 air fryer baskets, and roast for 10 minutes. Stir the mixture well, then continue roasting for an additional 10 minutes. 4. Remove from the air fryer, transfer to a serving bowl, and enjoy.

Prawns Egg Rolls

Prep time: 15 minutes | Cook time: 10 minutes per batch | Serves 4

1 tablespoon mixed vegetables oil
½ head green or savoy cabbage, finely shredded
90 g grated carrots
240 ml canned bean sprouts, drained
1 tablespoon soy sauce
½ teaspoon sugar
1 teaspoon sesame oil
60 ml hoisin sauce
Freshly ground black pepper, to taste
454 g cooked prawns, diced
30 g spring onions
8 egg roll wrappers (or use spring roll pastry)
mixed vegetables oil
Duck sauce

1. Preheat a large sauté pan over medium-high heat. Add the oil and cook the cabbage, carrots and bean sprouts until they start to wilt, about 3 minutes. Add the soy sauce, sugar, sesame oil, hoisin sauce and black pepper. Sauté for a few more minutes. Stir in the prawns and spring onions and cook until the mixed vegetables are just tender. Transfer the mixture to a colander in a bowl to cool. Press or squeeze out any excess water from the filling so that you don't end up with soggy egg rolls. 2. Make the egg rolls: Place the egg roll wrappers on a flat surface with one of the points facing towards you so they look like diamonds. Dividing the filling evenly between the eight wrappers, spoon the mixture onto the centre of the egg roll wrappers. Spread the filling across the centre of the wrappers from the left corner to the right corner but leave 2 inches from each corner empty. Brush the empty sides of the wrapper with a little water. Fold the bottom corner of the wrapper tightly up over the filling, trying to avoid making any air pockets. Fold the left corner in toward the centre and then the right corner toward the centre. It should now look like an envelope. Tightly roll the egg roll from the bottom to the top open corner. Press to seal the egg roll together, brushing with a little extra water if need be. Repeat this technique with all 8 egg rolls. 3. Preheat the air fryer to 190ºC. 4. Spray or brush all sides of the egg rolls with mixed vegetables oil. Air fry 8 egg rolls at a time for 10 minutes, put them half in zone 1 and the remaining in zone 2, turning them over halfway through the cooking time. 5. Serve hot with duck sauce or your favourite dipping sauce.

Black Bean Corn Dip

Prep time: 10 minutes | Cook time: 10 minutes | Serves 4

½ (425 g) can black beans, drained and rinsed
½ (425 g) can sweetcorn, drained and rinsed
60 g chunky salsa
57 g low-fat soft white cheese
40 g shredded low-fat Cheddar cheese
½ teaspoon cumin powder
½ teaspoon paprika
Salt and freshly ground black pepper, to taste

Preheat the air fryer to 160ºC. 2. In a medium-sized bowl, mix together the black beans, sweetcorn, salsa, soft white cheese, Cheddar cheese, cumin, and paprika. Season with salt and pepper and stir until well combined. 3. Spoon the mixture into a baking dish. 4. Place baking dish in one of the air fryer baskets and bake until heated through, about 10 minutes. 5. Serve hot.

Stuffed Fried Mushrooms

Prep time: 20 minutes | Cook time: 10 to 11 minutes | Serves 10

50 g panko breadcrumbs
½ teaspoon freshly ground black pepper
½ teaspoon onion powder
½ teaspoon cayenne pepper
1 (227 g) package soft white cheese, at room temperature
20 cremini or button mushrooms, stemmed
1 to 2 tablespoons oil

1. In a medium-sized bowl, whisk the breadcrumbs, black pepper, onion powder, and cayenne until blended. 2. Add the soft white cheese and mix until well blended. Fill each mushroom top with 1 teaspoon of the soft white cheese mixture 3. Preheat the air fryer to 180ºC. Line 2 air fryer baskets with a piece of baking paper paper. 4. Place the mushrooms on the baking paper and spritz with oil. 5. Cook for 5 minutes. Shake the basket and cook for 5 to 6 minutes more until the filling is firm and the mushrooms are soft.

Spicy Tortilla Chips

Prep time: 5 minutes | Cook time: 8 to 12 minutes | Serves 4

½ teaspoon cumin powder
½ teaspoon paprika
½ teaspoon chili powder
½ teaspoon salt
Pinch cayenne pepper
8 (6-inch) sweetcorn tortillas, each cut into 6 wedges
Cooking spray

1. Preheat the air fryer to 190°C. Lightly spritz the air fryer basket with cooking spray. 2. Stir together the cumin, paprika, chili powder, salt, and pepper in a small bowl. 3. Working in batches, arrange the tortilla wedges in the air fryer baskets in a single layer. Lightly mist them with cooking spray. Sprinkle some seasoning mixture on top of the tortilla wedges. 4. Air fry for 4 to 6 minutes, shaking the basket halfway through, or until the chips are lightly browned and crunchy. 5. Repeat with the remaining tortilla wedges and seasoning mixture. 6. Let the tortilla chips cool for 5 minutes and serve.

Crispy Green Tomatoes with Horseradish

Prep time: 18 minutes | Cook time: 10 to 15 minutes | Serves 4

2 eggs
60 ml buttermilk
55 g breadcrumbs
75 g cornmeal
¼ teaspoon salt
680 g firm green tomatoes, cut into ¼-inch slices
Cooking spray
Horseradish Sauce:
60 ml soured cream
60 ml mayonnaise
2 teaspoons prepared horseradish
½ teaspoon lemon juice
½ teaspoon Worcestershire sauce
⅛ teaspoon black pepper

1. Preheat air fryer to 200°C. Spritz the air fryer basket with cooking spray. 2. In a small bowl, whisk together all the ingredients for the horseradish sauce until smooth. Set aside. 3. In a shallow dish, beat the eggs and buttermilk. 4. In a separate shallow dish, thoroughly combine the breadcrumbs, cornmeal, and salt. 5. Dredge the tomato slices, one at a time, in the egg mixture, then roll in the bread crumb mixture until evenly coated. 6. Working in batches, place the tomato slices in the air fryer basket in a single layer. Spray them with cooking spray. 7. Air fry for 10 to 15 minutes, flipping the slices halfway through, or until the tomato slices are nicely browned and crisp. 8. Remove from the basket to a platter and repeat with the remaining tomato slices. 9. Serve drizzled with the prepared horseradish sauce.

String Bean Fries

Prep time: 15 minutes | Cook time: 5 to 6 minutes | Serves 4

227 g fresh French beans
2 eggs
4 teaspoons water
60 g plain flour
50 g breadcrumbs
¼ teaspoon salt
¼ teaspoon ground black pepper
¼ teaspoon mustard powder (optional)
Oil for misting or cooking spray

1. Preheat the air fryer to 180°C. 2. Trim stem ends from French beans, wash, and pat dry. 3. In a shallow dish, beat eggs and water together until well blended. 4. Place flour in a second shallow dish. 5. In a third shallow dish, stir together the breadcrumbs, salt, pepper, and mustard powder if using. 6. Dip each bean in egg mixture, flour, egg mixture again, then breadcrumbs. 7. When you finish coating all the French beans, open air fryer and place them in one basket. 8. Cook for 3 minutes. 9. Stop and mist French beans with oil or cooking spray. 10. Cook for 2 to 3 more minutes or until French beans are crispy and nicely browned.

Italian Rice Balls

Prep time: 20 minutes | Cook time: 10 minutes | Makes 8 rice balls

355 g cooked sticky rice
½ teaspoon Italian seasoning blend
¾ teaspoon salt, divided
8 black olives, pitted
28 g mozzarella cheese cheese,
cut into tiny pieces (small enough to stuff into olives)
2 eggs
35 g Italian breadcrumbs
55 g panko breadcrumbs
Cooking spray

1. Preheat air fryer to 200°C. 2. Stuff each black olive with a piece of mozzarella cheese cheese. Set aside. 3. In a bowl, combine the cooked sticky rice, Italian seasoning blend, and ½ teaspoon of salt and stir to mix well. Form the rice mixture into a log with your hands and divide it into 8 equal portions. Mould each portion around a black olive and roll into a ball. 4. Transfer to the freezer to chill for 10 to 15 minutes until firm. 5. In a shallow dish, place the Italian breadcrumbs. In a separate shallow dish, whisk the eggs. In a third shallow dish, combine the panko breadcrumbs and remaining salt. 6. One by one, roll the rice balls in the Italian breadcrumbs, then dip in the whisked eggs, finally coat them with the panko breadcrumbs. 7. Arrange the rice balls in both zone 1 and zone 2 and spritz both sides with cooking spray. 8. Air fry for 10 minutes until the rice balls are golden. Flip the balls halfway through the cooking time. 9. Serve warm.

50 | Chapter 7 Snacks and Appetizers

Cheese Drops

Prep time: 15 minutes | Cook time: 10 minutes per batch | Serves 8

90 g plain flour
½ teaspoon rock salt
¼ teaspoon cayenne pepper
¼ teaspoon smoked paprika
¼ teaspoon black pepper
a dash of garlic powder (optional)
57 g butter, softened
100 g grated extra mature cheddar cheese, at room temperature
Olive oil spray

1. In a small bowl, combine the flour, salt, cayenne, paprika, pepper, and garlic powder, if using. 2. Using a food processor, cream the butter and cheese until smooth. Gently add the seasoned flour and process until the dough is well combined, smooth, and no longer sticky. (Or make the dough in a stand mixer fitted with the paddle attachment: Cream the butter and cheese at medium speed until smooth, then add the seasoned flour and beat at low speed until smooth.) 3. Divide the dough into 32 pieces of equal size. On a lightly floured surface, roll each piece into a small ball. 4. Spray the air fryer basket with oil spray. Arrange cheese drops half in zone 1, the remaining in zone 2. In zone 1, Set the air fryer to 160ºC for 10 minutes, or until drops are just starting to brown. In zone 2, select Match Cook and press Start. Transfer to a a wire rack. If necessary, repeat with remaining dough, checking for degree of doneness at 8 minutes. 5. Cool the cheese drops completely on the a wire rack. Store in an airtight container until ready to serve, or up to 1 or 2 days.

Bacon-Wrapped Prawns and Jalapeño Chillies

Prep time: 20 minutes | Cook time: 26 minutes | Serves 8

24 large prawns, peeled and deveined, about 340 g
5 tablespoons barbecue sauce, divided
12 strips bacon, cut in half
24 small pickled jalapeño chillies slices

1. Toss together the prawns and 3 tablespoons of the barbecue sauce. Let stand for 15 minutes. Soak 24 wooden cocktail sticks in water for 10 minutes. Wrap 1 piece bacon around the prawns and jalapeño chillies slice, then secure with a cocktail stick. 2. Preheat the air fryer to 180ºC. 3. Place half of the prawns in zone 1, the remaining in zone 2, spacing them ½ inch apart. In zone 1, select Air Fry button, set the time to 3 minutes or more, or until bacon is golden and prawns are fully cooked. In zone 2, select Match Cook and then press Start. If necessary, work in batches. 4. Brush with the remaining barbecue sauce and serve.

Dark Chocolate and Cranberry Granola Bars

Prep time: 5 minutes | Cook time: 15 minutes | Serves 6

135 g certified gluten-free quick oats
2 tablespoons sugar-free dark chocolate chunks
2 tablespoons unsweetened dried cranberries
3 tablespoons unsweetened shredded coconut
120 ml raw honey
1 teaspoon cinnamon powder
⅛ teaspoon salt
2 tablespoons olive oil

1. Preheat the air fryer to 180ºC. Line an 8-by-8-inch baking dish with baking paper paper that comes up the side so you can lift it out after cooking. 2. In a large bowl, mix together all of the ingredients until well combined. 3. Press the oat mixture into the pan in an even layer. 4. Place the pan into the air fryer basket and bake for 15 minutes. 5. Remove the pan from the air fryer and lift the granola cake out of the pan using the edges of the baking paper paper. 6. Allow to cool for 5 minutes before slicing into 6 equal bars. 7. Serve immediately or wrap in plastic wrap and store at room temperature for up to 1 week.

Mixed Vegetables Pot Stickers

Prep time: 12 minutes | Cook time: 11 to 18 minutes | Makes 12 pot stickers

70 g shredded red cabbage
25 g chopped button mushrooms
35 g grated carrot
2 tablespoons minced onion
2 garlic cloves, minced
2 teaspoons grated fresh ginger
12 gyoza/pot sticker wrappers
2½ teaspoons olive oil, divided

1. In a baking pan, combine the red cabbage, mushrooms, carrot, onion, garlic, and ginger. Add 1 tablespoon of water. Place in the air fryer and air fry at 190ºC for 3 to 6 minutes, until the mixed vegetables are crisp-tender. Drain and set aside. 2. Working one at a time, place the pot sticker wrappers on a work surface. Top each wrapper with a scant 1 tablespoon of the filling. Fold half of the wrapper over the other half to form a half circle. Dab one edge with water and press both edges together. 3. To another pan, add 1¼ teaspoons of olive oil. Put half of the pot stickers, seam-side up, in the pan. Air fry for 5 minutes, or until the bottoms are light golden. Add 1 tablespoon of water and return the pan to the air fryer. 4. Air fry for 4 to 6 minutes more, or until hot. Repeat with the remaining pot stickers, remaining 1¼ teaspoons of oil, and another tablespoon of water. Serve immediately.

Fried Artichoke Hearts

Prep time: 10 minutes | Cook time: 12 minutes | Serves 10

Oil, for spraying
3 (397 g) cans quartered artichokes, drained and patted dry
120 ml mayonnaise
180 g panko breadcrumbs
50 g grated Parmesan cheese
Salt and freshly ground black pepper, to taste

1. Line the air fryer basket with baking paper and spray lightly with oil. 2. Place the artichokes on a plate. Put the mayonnaise and breadcrumbs in separate bowls. 3. Working one at a time, dredge each artichoke heart in the mayonnaise, then in the breadcrumbs to cover. 4. Place the artichokes in the prepared basket, half in zone 1 and the remaining in zone 2. You may need to work in batches, depending on the size of your air fryer. 5. Air fry at 190ºC for 10 to 12 minutes, or until crispy and golden. 6. Sprinkle with the Parmesan cheese and season with salt and black pepper. Serve immediately.

Prawns Toasts with Sesame Seeds

Prep time: 15 minutes | Cook time: 6 to 8 minutes | Serves 4 to 6

230 g raw prawns, peeled and deveined
1 egg, beaten
2 spring onions, chopped, plus more for garnish
2 tablespoons finely chopped fresh coriander
2 teaspoons grated fresh ginger
1 to 2 teaspoons sriracha sauce
1 teaspoon soy sauce
½ teaspoon toasted sesame oil
6 slices thinly sliced white sandwich bread
75 g sesame seeds
Cooking spray
Thai chilli sauce, for serving

1. Preheat the air fryer to 200ºC. Spritz the air fryer basket with cooking spray. 2. In a food processor, add the prawns, egg, spring onions, coriander, ginger, sriracha sauce, soy sauce and sesame oil, and pulse until chopped finely. You'll need to stop the food processor occasionally to scrape down the sides. Transfer the prawns mixture to a bowl. 3. On a clean work surface, cut the crusts off the sandwich bread. Using a brush, generously brush one side of each slice of bread with prawns mixture. 4. Place the sesame seeds on a plate. Press bread slices, prawns-side down, into sesame seeds to coat evenly. Cut each slice diagonally into quarters. 5. Spread the coated slices in a single layer in both zone 1 and zone 2. 6. Air fry in batches for 6 to 8 minutes, or until golden and crispy. Flip the bread slices halfway through. Repeat with the remaining bread slices. 7. Transfer to a plate and let cool for 5 minutes. Top with the chopped spring onions and serve warm with Thai chilli sauce.

Root Veggie Chips with Herb Salt & Grilled Ham and Cheese on Raisin Bread

Prep time: 15 minutes | Cook time: 10 minutes

Root Veggie Chips with Herb Salt | Serves 2:

1 parsnip, washed
1 small beetroot, washed
1 small turnip, washed
½ small sweet potato, washed
1 teaspoon olive oil
Cooking spray
Herb Salt:
¼ teaspoon rock salt
2 teaspoons finely chopped fresh parsley

Grilled Ham and Cheese on Raisin Bread | Serves 1:

2 slices raisin bread or fruit loaf
2 tablespoons butter, softened
2 teaspoons honey mustard
3 slices thinly sliced honey roast ham (about 85 g)
4 slices Muenster cheese (about 85 g)
2 cocktail sticks

Prepare for Root Veggie Chips with Herb Salt:

1. Preheat the air fryer to 180ºC on zone 1 drawer.
2. Peel and thinly slice the parsnip, beetroot, turnip, and sweet potato, then place the mixed vegetables in a large bowl, add the olive oil, and toss.
3. Spray the air fryer basket with cooking spray, then place the mixed vegetables in zone 1 drawer.

Prepare for Grilled Ham and Cheese on Raisin Bread:

Cook:

1. In zone 1, set the temperature to 180ºC, set the time to 8 minutes.
2. In zone 2, set the temperature to 190ºC, set the time to 5 minutes.
3. Press SYNC, then press Start.
4. While the chips cook, make the herb salt in a small bowl by combining the rock salt and parsley. Remove the chips and place on a serving plate, then sprinkle the herb salt on top and allow to cool for 2 to 3 minutes before serving.
5. Flip the sandwich over, remove the cocktail sticks and air fry for another 5 minutes. Cut the sandwich in half and enjoy!

Prawns Pirogues

Prep time: 15 minutes | Cook time: 4 to 5 minutes | Serves 8

340 g small, peeled, and deveined raw prawns
85 g soft white cheese, at room temperature
2 tablespoons natural yoghurt
1 teaspoon lemon juice
1 teaspoon dried fresh dill weed weed, crushed
Salt, to taste
4 small English cucumbers, each approximately 6 inches long

1. Pour 4 tablespoons water in bottom of air fryer drawer. 2. Place prawns half in zone 1, the remaining in zone 2 in single layer and air fry at 200ºC for 4 to 5 minutes, just until done. Watch carefully because prawns cooks quickly, and overcooking makes it tough. 3. Chop prawns into small pieces, no larger than ½ inch. Refrigerate while mixing the remaining ingredients. 4. With a fork, mash and whip the soft white cheese until smooth. 5. Stir in the yoghurt and beat until smooth. Stir in lemon juice, fresh dill weed, and chopped prawns. 6. Taste for seasoning. If needed, add ¼ to ½ teaspoon salt to suit your taste. 7. Store in refrigerator until serving time. 8. When ready to serve, wash and dry cucumbers and split them lengthwise. Scoop out the seeds and turn cucumbers upside down on kitchen roll to drain for 10 minutes. 9. Just before filling, wipe centres of cucumbers dry. Spoon the prawns mixture into the pirogues and cut in half crosswise. Serve immediately.

Chapter 8 Vegetables and Sides

Chapter 8 Vegetables and Sides

Broccoli with Sesame Dressing

Prep time: 5 minutes | Cook time: 10 minutes | Serves 4

425 g broccoli florets, cut into bite-size pieces
1 tablespoon olive oil
¼ teaspoon salt
2 tablespoons sesame seeds
2 tablespoons rice vinegar
2 tablespoons coconut aminos
2 tablespoons sesame oil
½ teaspoon xylitol
¼ teaspoon red pepper flakes (optional)

1. Preheat the air fryer to 200°C. 2. In a large bowl, toss the broccoli with the olive oil and salt until thoroughly coated. 3. Transfer the broccoli to one of the air fryer baskets. Pausing halfway through the cooking time to shake the basket, air fry for 10 minutes until the stems are tender and the edges are beginning to crisp. 4. Meanwhile, in the same large bowl, whisk together the sesame seeds, vinegar, coconut aminos, sesame oil, xylitol, and red pepper flakes (if using). 5. Transfer the broccoli to the bowl and toss until thoroughly coated with the seasonings. Serve warm or at room temperature.

Golden Pickles

Prep time: 10 minutes | Cook time: 15 minutes | Serves 4

14 dill pickles, sliced
30 g flour
⅛ teaspoon baking powder
Pinch of salt
2 tablespoons cornflour plus 3
tablespoons water
6 tablespoons panko bread crumbs
½ teaspoon paprika
Cooking spray

1. Preheat the air fryer to 200°C. 2. Drain any excess moisture out of the dill pickles on a paper towel. 3. In a bowl, combine the flour, baking powder and salt. 4. Throw in the cornflour and water mixture and combine well with a whisk. 5. Put the panko bread crumbs in a shallow dish along with the paprika. Mix thoroughly. 6. Dip the pickles in the flour batter, before coating in the bread crumbs. Spritz all the pickles with the cooking spray. 7. Transfer to one of the air fryer baskets and air fry for 15 minutes, or until golden brown. 8. Serve immediately.

Chermoula-Roasted Beetroots

Prep time: 15 minutes | Cook time: 25 minutes | Serves 4

Chermoula:

30 g packed fresh coriander leaves
15 g packed fresh parsley leaves
6 cloves garlic, peeled
2 teaspoons smoked paprika
2 teaspoons ground cumin
1 teaspoon ground coriander
½ to 1 teaspoon cayenne pepper
Pinch crushed saffron (optional)
115 g extra-virgin olive oil
coarse sea salt, to taste

Beetroots:

3 medium beetroots, trimmed, peeled, and cut into 1-inch chunks
2 tablespoons chopped fresh coriander
2 tablespoons chopped fresh parsley

1. For the chermoula: In a food processor, combine the fresh coriander, parsley, garlic, paprika, cumin, ground coriander, and cayenne. Pulse until coarsely chopped. Add the saffron, if using, and process until combined. With the food processor running, slowly add the olive oil in a steady stream; process until the sauce is uniform. Season to taste with salt. 2. For the beetroots: In a large bowl, drizzle the beetroots with ½ cup of the chermoula, or enough to coat. Arrange the beetroots in the air fryer basket. Set the air fryer to 190°C for 25 to minutes, or until the beetroots are tender. 3. Transfer the beetroots to a serving platter. Sprinkle with chopped coriander and parsley and serve.

Roasted Radishes with Sea Salt

Prep time: 5 minutes | Cook time: 18 minutes | Serves 4

450 g radishes, ends trimmed if needed
2 tablespoons olive oil
½ teaspoon sea salt

1. Preheat the air fryer to 180°C. 2. In a large bowl, combine the radishes with olive oil and sea salt. 3. Pour the radishes into the air fryer and roast for 10 minutes. Stir or turn the radishes over and roast for 8 minutes more, then serve.

Parmesan-Rosemary Radishes

Prep time: 5 minutes | Cook time: 15 to 20 minutes | Serves 4

1 bunch radishes, stemmed, trimmed, and quartered
1 tablespoon avocado oil
2 tablespoons finely grated fresh Parmesan cheese
1 tablespoon chopped fresh rosemary
Sea salt and freshly ground black pepper, to taste

1. Place the radishes in a medium bowl and toss them with the avocado oil, Parmesan cheese, rosemary, salt, and pepper. 2. Set the air fryer to 190°C. Arrange the radishes in a single layer in zone 1 drawer. Roast for 15 to 20 minutes, until golden brown and tender. Let cool for 5 minutes before serving.

Mashed Sweet Potato Tots

Prep time: 10 minutes | Cook time: 12 to 13 minutes per batch | Makes 18 to 24 tots

210 g cooked mashed sweet potatoes
1 egg white, beaten
⅛ teaspoon ground cinnamon
1 dash nutmeg
2 tablespoons chopped pecans
1½ teaspoons honey
Salt, to taste
50 g panko bread crumbs
Oil for misting or cooking spray

1. Preheat the air fryer to 200°C. 2. In a large bowl, mix together the potatoes, egg white, cinnamon, nutmeg, pecans, honey, and salt to taste. 3. Place panko crumbs on a sheet of wax paper. 4. For each tot, use about 2 teaspoons of sweet potato mixture. To shape, drop the measure of potato mixture onto panko crumbs and push crumbs up and around potatoes to coat edges. Then turn tot over to coat other side with crumbs. 5. Mist tots with oil or cooking spray and place half in zone 1, the remaining in zone 2 in single layer. 6. Air fry at 200°C for 12 to 13 minutes, until browned and crispy. 7. Repeat steps 5 and 6 to cook remaining tots.

Broccoli-Cheddar Twice-Baked Potatoes

Prep time: 10 minutes | Cook time: 46 minutes | Serves 4

Oil, for spraying
2 medium Maris Piper potatoes
1 tablespoon olive oil
30 g broccoli florets
1 tablespoon sour cream
1 teaspoon garlic powder
1 teaspoon onion powder
60 g shredded Cheddar cheese

1. Line the air fryer baskets with parchment and spray lightly with oil. 2. Rinse the potatoes and pat dry with paper towels. Rub the outside of the potatoes with the olive oil and place them in the prepared baskets. 3. Air fry at 200°C for 40 minutes, or until easily pierced with a fork. Let cool just enough to handle, then cut the potatoes in half lengthwise. 4. Meanwhile, place the broccoli in a microwave-safe bowl, cover with water, and microwave on high for 5 to 8 minutes. Drain and set aside. 5. Scoop out most of the potato flesh and transfer to a medium bowl. 6. Add the sour cream, garlic, and onion powder and stir until the potatoes are mashed. 7. Spoon the potato mixture back into the hollowed potato skins, mounding it to fit, if necessary. Top with the broccoli and cheese. Return the potatoes to the baskets. You may need to work in batches, depending on the size of your air fryer. 8. Air fry at 200°C for 3 to 6 minutes, or until the cheese has melted. Serve immediately.

Rosemary New Potatoes

Prep time: 10 minutes | Cook time: 5 to 6 minutes | Serves 4

3 large red potatoes
¼ teaspoon ground rosemary
¼ teaspoon ground thyme
⅛ teaspoon salt
⅛ teaspoon ground black pepper
2 teaspoons extra-light olive oil

1. Preheat the air fryer to 170°C. 2. Place potatoes in large bowl and sprinkle with rosemary, thyme, salt, and pepper. 3. Stir with a spoon to distribute seasonings evenly. 4. Add oil to potatoes and stir again to coat well. 5. Air fry at 170°C for 4 minutes. Stir and break apart any that have stuck together. 6. Cook an additional 1 to 2 minutes or until fork-tender.

Stuffed Red Peppers with Herbed Ricotta and Tomatoes

Prep time: 10 minutes | Cook time: 20 minutes | Serves 4

2 red peppers
250 g cooked brown rice
2 plum tomatoes, diced
1 garlic clove, minced
¼ teaspoon salt
¼ teaspoon black pepper
115 g ricotta
3 tablespoons fresh basil, chopped
3 tablespoons fresh oregano, chopped
20 g shredded Parmesan, for topping

1. Preheat the air fryer to 180°C. 2. Cut the bell peppers in half and remove the seeds and stem. 3. In a medium bowl, combine the brown rice, tomatoes, garlic, salt, and pepper. 4. Distribute the rice filling evenly among the four bell pepper halves. 5. In a small bowl, combine the ricotta, basil, and oregano. Put the herbed cheese over the top of the rice mixture in each bell pepper. 6. Place the bell peppers into the air fryer and roast for 20 minutes. 7. Remove and serve with shredded Parmesan on top.

Crispy Green Beans

Prep time: 5 minutes | Cook time: 8 minutes | Serves 4

2 teaspoons olive oil
230 g fresh green beans, ends trimmed
¼ teaspoon salt
¼ teaspoon ground black pepper

1. In a large bowl, drizzle olive oil over green beans and sprinkle with salt and pepper. 2. Place green beans into ungreased air fryer basket. Adjust the temperature to 180°C and set the timer for 8 minutes, shaking the basket two times during cooking. Green beans will be dark golden and crispy at the edges when done. Serve warm.

Burger Bun for One & Cheddar Broccoli with Bacon

Prep time: 12 minutes | Cook time: 10 minutes

Burger Bun for One | Serves 1:

2 tablespoons salted butter, melted
25 g blanched finely ground almond flour
¼ teaspoon baking powder
⅛ teaspoon apple cider vinegar
1 large egg, whisked

Cheddar Broccoli with Bacon | Serves 2:

215 g fresh broccoli florets
1 tablespoon coconut oil
115 g shredded sharp Cheddar cheese
60 g full-fat sour cream
4 slices sugar-free bacon, cooked and crumbled
1 spring onion, sliced on the bias

Prepare for Burger Bun for One:

1. Pour butter into an ungreased ramekin. Add flour, baking powder, and vinegar to ramekin and stir until combined. Add egg and stir until batter is mostly smooth.
2. Place ramekin into zone 1 drawer.

Prepare for Cheddar Broccoli with Bacon:

1. Place broccoli into zone 2 drawer and drizzle it with coconut oil.

Cook:

1. In zone 1, set the temperature to 180°C, set the time to 5 minutes. Work in batches if necessary.
2. In zone 2, set the temperature to 180°C, set the time to 10 minutes.
3. Press SYNC, then press Start.
4. For zone 1, when done, the centre will be firm and the top slightly browned. Let cool, about 5 minutes, then remove from ramekin and slice in half. Serve.
5. For zone 2, toss the basket two or three times during cooking to avoid burned spots. When broccoli begins to crisp at ends, remove from fryer. Top with shredded cheese, sour cream, and crumbled bacon and garnish with spring onion slices.

Cheesy Loaded Broccoli & Corn and Coriander Salad

Prep time: 20 minutes | Cook time: 10 minutes

Cheesy Loaded Broccoli | Serves 2

215 g fresh broccoli florets
1 tablespoon coconut oil
¼ teaspoon salt
120 g shredded sharp Cheddar cheese
60 g sour cream
4 slices cooked sugar-free bacon, crumbled
1 medium spring onion, trimmed and sliced on the bias

Corn and Coriander Salad | Serves 2

2 ears of corn, shucked (halved crosswise if too large to fit in your air fryer)
1 tablespoon unsalted butter, at room temperature
1 teaspoon chili powder
¼ teaspoon garlic powder
coarse sea salt and freshly ground black pepper, to taste
20 g lightly packed fresh coriander leaves
1 tablespoon sour cream
1 tablespoon mayonnaise
1 teaspoon adobo sauce (from a can of chipotle peppers in adobo sauce)
2 tablespoons crumbled feta cheese
Lime wedges, for serving

Prepare for Cheesy Loaded Broccoli:

1. Place broccoli into ungreased zone 1 drawer, drizzle with coconut oil, and sprinkle with salt.

Prepare for Corn and Coriander Salad:

1. Brush the corn all over with the butter, then sprinkle with the chili powder and garlic powder, and season with salt and pepper.
2. Place the corn in zone 2 drawer.

Cook:

1. In zone 1, set the temperature to 180°C, set the time to 8 minutes. Shake basket three times during cooking to avoid burned spots.
2. In zone 2, set the temperature to 200°C, set the time to 10 minutes, turning over halfway through, until the kernels are lightly charred and tender.
3. Press SYNC, then press Start.
4. Sprinkle broccoli with Cheddar and cook for 2 additional minutes. When done, cheese will be melted and broccoli will be tender. Serve warm in a large serving dish, topped with sour cream, crumbled bacon, and spring onion slices.
5. Transfer the ears to a cutting board, let stand 1 minute, then carefully cut the kernels off the cobs and move them to a bowl. Add the coriander leaves and toss to combine (the coriander leaves will wilt slightly). In a small bowl, stir together the sour cream, mayonnaise, and adobo sauce. Divide the corn and coriander among plates and spoon the adobo dressing over the top. Sprinkle with the feta cheese and serve with lime wedges on the side.

Bacon Potatoes and Green Beans

Prep time: 10 minutes | Cook time: 25 minutes | Serves 4

Oil, for spraying
900 g medium Maris Piper potatoes, quartered
100 g bacon bits
280 g fresh green beans
1 teaspoon salt
½ teaspoon freshly ground black pepper

1. Line one of the air fryer baskets with parchment and spray lightly with oil. 2. Place the potatoes in the prepared basket. Top with the bacon bits and green beans. Sprinkle with the salt and black pepper and spray liberally with oil. 3. Air fry at 180°C for 25 minutes, stirring after 12 minutes and spraying with oil, until the potatoes are easily pierced with a fork.

Roasted Grape Tomatoes and Asparagus

Prep time: 5 minutes | Cook time: 12 minutes | Serves 6

400 g grape tomatoes
1 bunch asparagus, trimmed
2 tablespoons olive oil
3 garlic cloves, minced
½ teaspoon coarse sea salt

1. Preheat the air fryer to 190°C. 2. In a large bowl, combine all of the ingredients, tossing until the vegetables are well coated with oil. 3. Pour the vegetable mixture half in zone 1, the remaining in zone 2 and spread into a single layer, then roast for 12 minutes.

Asian Tofu Salad

Prep time: 25 minutes | Cook time: 15 minutes | Serves 2

Tofu:

1 tablespoon soy sauce
1 tablespoon vegetable oil
1 teaspoon minced fresh ginger
1 teaspoon minced garlic
230 g extra-firm tofu, drained and cubed

Salad:

60 ml rice vinegar
1 tablespoon sugar
1 teaspoon salt
1 teaspoon black pepper
25 g sliced spring onions
120 g julienned cucumber
50 g julienned red onion
130 g julienned carrots
6 butter lettuce leaves

1. For the tofu: In a small bowl, whisk together the soy sauce, vegetable oil, ginger, and garlic. Add the tofu and mix gently. Let stand at room temperature for 10 minutes. 2. Arrange the tofu in a single layer in zone 1 drawer. Set the air fryer to 200°C for 15 minutes, shaking halfway through the cooking time. 3. Meanwhile, for the salad: In a large bowl, whisk together the vinegar, sugar, salt, pepper, and spring onions. Add the cucumber, onion, and carrots and toss to combine. Set aside to marinate while the tofu cooks. 4. To serve, arrange three lettuce leaves on each of two plates. Pile the marinated vegetables (and marinade) on the lettuce. Divide the tofu between the plates and serve.

Parmesan Mushrooms

Prep time: 5 minutes | Cook time: 15 minutes | Serves 4

Oil, for spraying
450 g shitake mushrooms, stems trimmed
2 tablespoons olive oil
2 teaspoons granulated garlic
1 teaspoon onion powder
½ teaspoon salt
¼ teaspoon freshly ground black pepper
30 g grated Parmesan cheese, divided

1. Line one of the air fryer baskets with parchment and spray lightly with oil. 2. In a large bowl, toss the mushrooms with the olive oil, garlic, onion powder, salt, and black pepper until evenly coated. 3. Place the mushrooms in the prepared basket. 4. Roast at 190°C for 13 minutes. 5. Sprinkle half of the cheese over the mushrooms and cook for another 2 minutes. 6. Transfer the mushrooms to a serving bowl, add the remaining Parmesan cheese, and toss until evenly coated. Serve immediately.

Hawaiian Brown Rice

Prep time: 10 minutes | Cook time: 12 to 16 minutes | Serves 4 to 6

110 g ground sausage
1 teaspoon butter
20 g minced onion
40 g minced bell pepper
380 g cooked brown rice
1 (230 g) can crushed pineapple, drained

1. Shape sausage into 3 or 4 thin patties. Air fry at 200°C for 6 to 8 minutes or until well done. Remove from air fryer, drain, and crumble. Set aside. 2. Place butter, onion, and bell pepper in baking pan. Roast at 200°C for 1 minute and stir. Cook 3 to 4 minutes longer or just until vegetables are tender. 3. Add sausage, rice, and pineapple to vegetables and stir together. 4. Roast for 2 to 3 minutes, until heated through.

Brussels Sprouts with Pecans and Gorgonzola

Prep time: 10 minutes | Cook time: 25 minutes | Serves 4

65 g pecans	Salt and freshly ground black pepper, to taste
680 g fresh Brussels sprouts, trimmed and quartered	30 g crumbled Gorgonzola cheese
2 tablespoons olive oil	

1. Spread the pecans in a single layer of the air fryer and set the heat to 180ºC. Air fry for 3 to 5 minutes until the pecans are lightly browned and fragrant. Transfer the pecans to a plate and continue preheating the air fryer, increasing the heat to 200ºC. 2. In a large bowl, toss the Brussels sprouts with the olive oil and season with salt and black pepper to taste. 3. Working in batches if necessary, arrange the Brussels sprouts in a single layer half in zone 1, the remaining in zone 2. Pausing halfway through the baking time to shake the basket, air fry for 20 to 25 minutes until the sprouts are tender and starting to brown on the edges. 4. Transfer the sprouts to a serving bowl and top with the toasted pecans and Gorgonzola. Serve warm or at room temperature.

Green Peas with Mint

Prep time: 5 minutes | Cook time: 5 minutes | Serves 4

75 g shredded lettuce	1 tablespoon fresh mint, shredded
1 (280 g) package frozen green peas, thawed	1 teaspoon melted butter

1. Lay the shredded lettuce in one of the air fryer baskets. 2. Toss together the peas, mint, and melted butter and spoon over the lettuce. 3. Air fry at 180ºC for 5 minutes, until peas are warm and lettuce wilts.

Glazed Sweet Potato Bites

Prep time: 10 minutes | Cook time: 25 minutes | Serves 4

Oil, for spraying	2 tablespoons honey
3 medium sweet potatoes, peeled and cut into 1-inch pieces	1 tablespoon olive oil
	2 teaspoons ground cinnamon

1. Line one of the air fryer baskets with parchment and spray lightly with oil. 2. In a large bowl, toss together the sweet potatoes, honey, olive oil, and cinnamon until evenly coated. 3. Place the potatoes in the prepared basket. 4. Air fry at 200ºC for 20 to 25 minutes, or until crispy and easily pierced with a fork.

Crispy Courgette Sticks

Prep time: 5 minutes | Cook time: 14 minutes | Serves 4

2 small courgette, cut into 2-inch × ½-inch sticks	¼ teaspoon sea salt
3 tablespoons chickpea flour	⅛ teaspoon freshly ground black pepper
2 teaspoons arrowroot (or cornflour)	1 tablespoon water
½ teaspoon garlic granules	Cooking spray

1. Preheat the air fryer to 200ºC. 2. Combine the courgette sticks with the chickpea flour, arrowroot, garlic granules, salt, and pepper in a medium bowl and toss to coat. Add the water and stir to mix well. 3. Spritz one of the air fryer baskets with cooking spray and spread out the courgette sticks in the basket. Mist the courgette sticks with cooking spray. 4. Air fry for 14 minutes, shaking the basket halfway through, or until the courgette sticks are crispy and nicely browned. 5. Serve warm.

Dinner Rolls

Prep time: 10 minutes | Cook time: 12 minutes | Serves 6

225 g shredded Mozzarella cheese	almond flour
30 g full-fat cream cheese	40 g ground flaxseed
95 g blanched finely ground	½ teaspoon baking powder
	1 large egg

1. Place Mozzarella, cream cheese, and almond flour in a large microwave-safe bowl. Microwave for 1 minute. Mix until smooth. 2. Add flaxseed, baking powder, and egg until fully combined and smooth. Microwave an additional 15 seconds if it becomes too firm. 3. Separate the dough into six pieces and roll into balls. Place the balls half in zone 1, the remaining in zone 2. 4. In zone 1, adjust the temperature to 160ºC and air fry for 12 minutes. In zone 2, select Match Cook and press Start. 5. Allow rolls to cool completely before serving.

Courgette Balls

Prep time: 5 minutes | Cook time: 10 minutes | Serves 4

4 courgettes
1 egg
45 g grated Parmesan cheese

1 tablespoon Italian herbs
75 g grated coconut

1. Thinly grate the courgettes and dry with a cheesecloth, ensuring to remove all the moisture. 2. In a bowl, combine the courgettes with the egg, Parmesan, Italian herbs, and grated coconut, mixing well to incorporate everything. Using the hands, mold the mixture into balls. 3. Preheat the air fryer to 200°C. 4. Lay the courgette balls in one of the air fryer baskets and air fry for 10 minutes. 5. Serve hot.

Chapter 9 Vegetarian Mains

Chapter 9 Vegetarian Mains

Crispy Tofu

Prep time: 30 minutes | Cook time: 15 to 20 minutes | Serves 4

1 (454 g) block extra-firm tofu
2 tablespoons coconut aminos
1 tablespoon toasted sesame oil
1 tablespoon olive oil
1 tablespoon chilli-garlic sauce
1½ teaspoons black sesame seeds
1 spring onion, thinly sliced

1. Press the tofu for at least 15 minutes by wrapping it in paper towels and setting a heavy pan on top so that the moisture drains. 2.Slice the tofu into bite-size cubes and transfer to a bowl. 3.Drizzle with the coconut aminos, sesame oil, olive oil, and chilli-garlic sauce. 4.Cover and refrigerate for 1 hour or up to overnight. 5.Preheat the air fryer to 200ºC. 6.Arrange the tofu in a single layer in one of the air fryer baskets. 7.Pausing to shake the pan halfway through the cooking time, air fry for 15 to 20 minutes until crisp. 8.Serve with any juices that accumulate in the bottom of the air fryer, sprinkled with the sesame seeds and sliced spring onion.

Roasted Vegetables with Rice

Prep time: 5 minutes | Cook time: 12 minutes | Serves 4

2 teaspoons melted butter
235 g chopped mushrooms
235 g cooked rice
235 g peas
1 carrot, chopped
1 red onion, chopped
1 garlic clove, minced
Salt and black pepper, to taste
2 hard-boiled eggs, grated
1 tablespoon soy sauce

1. Preheat the air fryer to 190ºC. 2.Coat a baking dish with melted butter. 3.Stir together the mushrooms, cooked rice, peas, carrot, onion, garlic, salt, and pepper in a large bowl until well mixed. 4.Pour the mixture into the prepared baking dish and transfer to one of the air fryer baskets. 5.Roast in the preheated air fryer for 12 minutes until the vegetables are tender. 6.Divide the mixture among four plates. 7.Serve warm with a sprinkle of grated eggs and a drizzle of soy sauce.

Caprese Aubergine Stacks

Prep time: 5 minutes | Cook time: 12 minutes | Serves 4

1 medium aubergine, cut into ¼-inch slices
2 large tomatoes, cut into ¼-inch slices
110 g fresh Mozzarella, cut into 14 g slices
2 tablespoons olive oil
60 g fresh basil, sliced

1. In a baking dish, place four slices of aubergine on the bottom. 2.Place a slice of tomato on top of each aubergine round, then Mozzarella, then aubergine. 3.Repeat as necessary. 4.Drizzle with olive oil. 5.Cover dish with foil and place dish into one of the air fryer baskets. 6.Adjust the temperature to 180ºC and bake for 12 minutes. 7.When done, aubergine will be tender. 8.Garnish with fresh basil to serve.

Cayenne Tahini Kale

Prep time: 5 minutes | Cook time: 15 minutes | Serves 2 to 4

Dressing:

60 ml tahini
60 g fresh lemon juice
2 tablespoons olive oil
1 teaspoon sesame seeds
½ teaspoon garlic powder
¼ teaspoon cayenne pepper

Kale:

1 Kg packed torn kale leaves (stems and ribs removed and leaves torn into palm-size pieces)
Rock salt and freshly ground black pepper, to taste

1. Preheat the air fryer to 180ºC. 2.Make the dressing: Whisk together the tahini, lemon juice, olive oil, sesame seeds, garlic powder, and cayenne pepper in a large bowl until well mixed. 3.Add the kale and massage the dressing thoroughly all over the leaves. 4.Sprinkle the salt and pepper to season. 5.Place the kale in one of the air fryer baskets in a single layer and air fry for about 15 minutes, or until the leaves are slightly wilted and crispy. 6.Remove from the basket and serve on a plate.

Courgette and Spinach Croquettes

Prep time: 9 minutes | Cook time: 7 minutes | Serves 6

4 eggs, slightly beaten	120 g Parmesan cheese, grated
120 g almond flour	⅓ teaspoon red pepper flakes
120 g goat cheese, crumbled	450 g courgette, peeled and grated
1 teaspoon fine sea salt	⅓ teaspoon dried dill weed
4 garlic cloves, minced	
235 g baby spinach	

1. Thoroughly combine all ingredients in a bowl. 2.Now, roll the mixture to form small croquettes. 3.Air fry at 170ºC for 7 minutes or until golden. 4.Tate, adjust for seasonings and serve warm.

Crispy Fried Okra with Chilli

Prep time: 5 minutes | Cook time: 10 minutes | Serves 4

3 tablespoons sour cream	Salt and black pepper, to taste
2 tablespoons flour	450 g okra, halved
2 tablespoons semolina	Cooking spray
½ teaspoon red chilli powder	

1. Preheat the air fryer to 200ºC. 2.Spray one of the air fryer baskets with cooking spray. 3.In a shallow bowl, place the sour cream. 4.In another shallow bowl, thoroughly combine the flour, semolina, red chilli powder, salt, and pepper. 5.Dredge the okra in the sour cream, then roll in the flour mixture until evenly coated. 6.Arrange the okra in the prepared basket and air fry for 10 minutes, flipping the okra halfway through, or until golden brown and crispy. 7.Cool for 5 minutes before serving.

Buffalo Cauliflower Bites with Blue Cheese

Prep time: 10 minutes | Cook time: 8 to 10 minutes | Serves 4

1 large head cauliflower, chopped into florets	120 ml mayonnaise
1 tablespoon olive oil	60 ml sour cream
Salt and freshly ground black pepper, to taste	2 tablespoons double cream
60 g unsalted butter, melted	1 tablespoon fresh lemon juice
60 ml hot sauce	1 clove garlic, minced
Garlic Blue Cheese Dip:	60 g crumbled blue cheese
	Salt and freshly ground black pepper, to taste

1. Preheat the air fryer to 200ºC. 2.In a large bowl, combine the cauliflower and olive oil. 3.Season to taste with salt and black pepper. 4.Toss until the vegetables are thoroughly coated. 5.Working in batches, place half of the cauliflower in zone 1, the remaining in zone 2. 6.Pausing halfway through the cooking time to shake the basket, air fry for 8 to 10 minutes until the cauliflower is evenly browned. 7.Transfer to a large bowl and repeat with the remaining cauliflower. 8.In a small bowl, whisk together the melted butter and hot sauce. 9.To make the dip: In a small bowl, combine the mayonnaise, sour cream, double cream, lemon juice, garlic, and blue cheese. 10.Season to taste with salt and freshly ground black pepper. 11.Just before serving, pour the butter mixture over the cauliflower and toss gently until thoroughly coated. 12.Serve with the dip on the side.

Parmesan Artichokes

Prep time: 10 minutes | Cook time: 10 minutes | Serves 4

2 medium artichokes, trimmed and quartered, centre removed	Parmesan cheese
2 tablespoons coconut oil	60 g blanched finely ground almond flour
1 large egg, beaten	½ teaspoon crushed red pepper flakes
120 g grated vegetarian	

1. In a large bowl, toss artichokes in coconut oil and then dip each piece into the egg. 2.Mix the Parmesan and almond flour in a large bowl. 3.Add artichoke pieces and toss to cover as completely as possible, sprinkle with pepper flakes. 4.Place into one of the air fryer baskets. 5.Adjust the temperature to 200ºC and air fry for 10 minutes. 6.Toss the basket two times during cooking. 7.Serve warm.

Whole Roasted Lemon Cauliflower

Prep time: 5 minutes | Cook time: 15 minutes | Serves 4

1 medium head cauliflower	1 medium lemon
2 tablespoons salted butter, melted	½ teaspoon garlic powder
	1 teaspoon dried parsley

1. Remove the leaves from the head of cauliflower and brush it with melted butter. 2.Cut the lemon in half and zest one half onto the cauliflower. 3.Squeeze the juice of the zested lemon half and pour it over the cauliflower. 4.Sprinkle with garlic powder and parsley. 5.Place cauliflower head into oen of the air fryer baskets. 6.Adjust the temperature to 180ºC and air fry for 15 minutes. 7.Check cauliflower every 5 minutes to avoid overcooking. 8.It should be fork tender. To serve, squeeze juice from other lemon half over cauliflower. 9.Serve immediately.

Broccoli with Garlic Sauce

Prep time: 19 minutes | Cook time: 15 minutes | Serves 4

2 tablespoons olive oil
Rock salt and freshly ground black pepper, to taste
450 g broccoli florets
Dipping Sauce:
2 teaspoons dried rosemary, crushed
3 garlic cloves, minced
⅓ teaspoon dried marjoram, crushed
60 ml sour cream
80 ml mayonnaise

1. Lightly grease your broccoli with a thin layer of olive oil. 2.Season with salt and ground black pepper. 3.Arrange the seasoned broccoli in one of the air fryer baskets. 4.Bake at 200°C for 15 minutes, shaking once or twice. 5.In the meantime, prepare the dipping sauce by mixing all the sauce ingredients. 6.Serve warm broccoli with the dipping sauce and enjoy!

Fried Root Vegetable Medley with Thyme

Prep time: 10 minutes | Cook time: 22 minutes | Serves 4

2 carrots, sliced
2 potatoes, cut into chunks
1 swede, cut into chunks
1 turnip, cut into chunks
1 beetroot, cut into chunks
8 shallots, halved
2 tablespoons olive oil
Salt and black pepper, to taste
2 tablespoons tomato pesto
2 tablespoons water
2 tablespoons chopped fresh thyme

1. Preheat the air fryer to 200°C. 2.Toss the carrots, potatoes, swede, turnip, beetroot, shallots, olive oil, salt, and pepper in a large mixing bowl until the root vegetables are evenly coated. 3.Place the root vegetables in one of the air fryer baskets and air fry for 12 minutes. 4.Shake the basket and air fry for another 10 minutes until they are cooked to your preferred doneness. 5.Meanwhile, in a small bowl, whisk together the tomato pesto and water until smooth. 6.When ready, remove the root vegetables from the basket to a platter. 7.Drizzle with the tomato pesto mixture and sprinkle with the thyme. 8.Serve immediately.

Cheese Stuffed Courgette

Prep time: 20 minutes | Cook time: 8 minutes | Serves 4

1 large courgette, cut into four pieces
2 tablespoons olive oil
235 g Ricotta cheese, room temperature
2 tablespoons spring onions, chopped
1 heaping tablespoon fresh parsley, roughly chopped
1 heaping tablespoon coriander, minced
60 g Cheddar cheese, preferably freshly grated
1 teaspoon celery seeds
½ teaspoon salt
½ teaspoon garlic pepper

1. Cook your courgette in the air fryer basket for approximately 10 minutes at 180°C. 2.Check for doneness and cook for 2-3 minutes longer if needed. 3.Meanwhile, make the stuffing by mixing the other items. 4.When your courgette is thoroughly cooked, open them up. 5.Divide the stuffing among all courgette pieces and bake an additional 5 minutes.

Chapter 10 Desserts

Chapter 10 Desserts

Grilled Pineapple Dessert

Prep time: 5 minutes | Cook time: 12 minutes | Serves 4

Coconut, or avocado oil for misting, or cooking spray
4 ½-inch-thick slices fresh pineapple, core removed
1 tablespoon honey
¼ teaspoon brandy, or apple juice
2 tablespoons slivered almonds, toasted
Vanilla frozen yogurt, coconut sorbet, or ice cream

1. Spray both sides of pineapple slices with oil or cooking spray. Place into one of air fryer baskets. 2. Air fry at 200ºC for 6 minutes. Turn slices over and cook for an additional 6 minutes. 3. Mix together the honey and brandy. 4. Remove cooked pineapple slices from air fryer, sprinkle with toasted almonds, and drizzle with honey mixture. 5. Serve with a scoop of frozen yogurt or sorbet on the side.

Brownies for Two

Prep time: 5 minutes | Cook time: 15 minutes | Serves 2

25g blanched finely ground almond flour
3 tablespoons granulated sweetener
3 tablespoons unsweetened cocoa powder
½ teaspoon baking powder
1 teaspoon vanilla extract
2 large eggs, whisked
2 tablespoons salted butter, melted

1. In a medium bowl, combine flour, sweetener, cocoa powder, and baking powder. 2. Add in vanilla, eggs, and butter, and stir until a thick batter forms. 3. Pour batter into two ramekins greased with cooking spray and place ramekins into zone 1 drawer. Adjust the temperature to 160ºC and bake for 15 minutes. Centers will be firm when done. Let ramekins cool 5 minutes before serving.

Baked Cheesecake

Prep time: 30 minutes | Cook time: 35 minutes | Serves 6

25 g almond flour
1½ tablespoons unsalted butter, melted
2 tablespoons granulated sweetener
225 g cream cheese, softened
15 g powdered sweetener
½ teaspoon vanilla paste
1 egg, at room temperature
Topping:
355 ml sour cream
3 tablespoons powdered sweetener
1 teaspoon vanilla extract

1. Thoroughly combine the almond flour, butter, and 2 tablespoons of granulated sweetener in a mixing bowl. Press the mixture into the bottom of lightly greased custard cups. 2. Then, mix the cream cheese, 25 g of powdered sweetener, vanilla, and egg using an electric mixer on low speed. Pour the batter into the pan, covering the crust. 3. Bake in the preheated air fryer at 160ºC for 35 minutes until edges are puffed and the surface is firm. 4. Mix the sour cream, 3 tablespoons of powdered sweetener, and vanilla for the topping; spread over the crust and allow it to cool to room temperature. 5. Transfer to your refrigerator for 6 to 8 hours. Serve well chilled.

Butter Flax Cookies

Prep time: 25 minutes | Cook time: 20 minutes | Serves 4

115 g almond meal
2 tablespoons flaxseed meal
30 g monk fruit, or equivalent sweetener
1 teaspoon baking powder
A pinch of grated nutmeg
A pinch of coarse salt
1 large egg, room temperature.
110 g unsalted butter, room temperature
1 teaspoon vanilla extract

1. Mix the almond meal, flaxseed meal, monk fruit, baking powder, grated nutmeg, and salt in a bowl. 2. In a separate bowl, whisk the egg, butter, and vanilla extract. 3. Stir the egg mixture into dry mixture; mix to combine well or until it forms a nice, soft dough. 4. Roll your dough out and cut out with a cookie cutter of your choice. Bake in the preheated air fryer at 180ºC for 10 minutes. Decrease the temperature to 160ºC and cook for 10 minutes longer. Bon appétit!

Apple Hand Pies

Prep time: 15 minutes | Cook time: 25 minutes | Serves 8

2 apples, cored and diced
60 ml honey
1 teaspoon ground cinnamon
1 teaspoon vanilla extract
⅛ teaspoon ground nutmeg
2 teaspoons cornflour
1 teaspoon water
1 sheet shortcrust pastry cut into 4
Cooking oil spray

1. Insert the crisper plate into the basket and the basket into the unit. Preheat the unit to 200ºC. 2. In a metal bowl that fits into the basket, stir together the apples, honey, cinnamon, vanilla, and nutmeg. 3. In a small bowl, whisk the cornflour and water until the cornflour dissolves. 4. Once the unit is preheated, place the metal bowl with the apples into the basket. 5. cook for 2 minutes then stir the apples. Resume cooking for 2 minutes. 6. Remove the bowl and stir the cornflour mixture into the apples. Reinsert the metal bowl into the basket and resume cooking for about 30 seconds until the sauce thickens slightly. 7. When the cooking is complete, refrigerate the apples while you prepare the piecrust. 8. Cut each piecrust into 2 (4-inch) circles. You should have 8 circles of crust. 9. Lay the piecrusts on a work surface. Divide the apple filling among the piecrusts, mounding the mixture in the center of each round. 10. Fold each piecrust over so the top layer of crust is about an inch short of the bottom layer. (The edges should not meet.) Use the back of a fork to seal the edges. 11. Insert the crisper plate into the baskets and the baskets into the unit. Preheat the unit 200ºC again. 12. Once the unit is preheated, spray the crisper plate with cooking oil, line the baskets with baking paper, and spray it with cooking oil. Working in batches, place the hand pies into the baskets in a single layer. 13. Cook the pies for 10 minutes. 14. When the cooking is complete, let the hand pies cool for 5 minutes before removing from the basket. 16. Repeat steps 12, 13, and 14 with the remaining pies.

Pumpkin Spice Pecans

Prep time: 5 minutes | Cook time: 6 minutes | Serves 4

125 g whole pecans
50 g granulated sweetener
1 large egg white
½ teaspoon ground cinnamon
½ teaspoon pumpkin pie spice
½ teaspoon vanilla extract

1. Toss all ingredients in a large bowl until pecans are coated. Place into one of the air fryer baskets. 2. Adjust the temperature to 150ºC and air fry for 6 minutes. 3. Toss two to three times during cooking. 4. Allow to cool completely. Store in an airtight container up to 3 days.

Mixed Berry Hand Pies

Prep time: 5 minutes | Cook time: 30 minutes | Serves 4

120 g granulated sugar
½ teaspoon ground cinnamon
1 tablespoon cornflour
150 g blueberries
150 g blackberries
150 g raspberries, divided into two equal portions
1 teaspoon water
1 package refrigerated shortcrust pastry (or your own homemade pastry)
1 egg, beaten

1. Combine the sugar, cinnamon, and cornstarch in a small saucepan. Add the blueberries, blackberries, and ½ of the raspberries. Toss the berries gently to coat them evenly. Add the teaspoon of water to the saucepan and turn the stovetop on to medium-high heat, stirring occasionally. Once the berries break down, release their juice, and start to simmer (about 5 minutes), simmer for another couple of minutes and then transfer the mixture to a bowl, stir in the remaining ½ of the raspberries and let it cool. 2. Preheat the air fryer to 190ºC. 3. Cut the pie dough into four 5-inch circles and four 6-inch circles. 4. Spread the 6-inch circles on a flat surface. Divide the berry filling between all four circles. Brush the perimeter of the dough circles with a little water. Place the 5-inch circles on top of the filling and press the perimeter of the dough circles together to seal. Roll the edges of the bottom circle up over the top circle to make a crust around the filling. Press a fork around the crust to make decorative indentations and to seal the crust shut. Brush the pies with egg wash and sprinkle a little sugar on top. Poke a small hole in the center of each pie with a paring knife to vent the dough. 5. Put the pies half in zone 1, the remaining in zone 2. If necessary, work in batches. Air fry for 9 minutes. Turn the pies over and air fry for another 6 minutes. Serve warm or at room temperature.

Vanilla Scones

Prep time: 20 minutes | Cook time: 10 minutes | Serves 6

55 g coconut flour
½ teaspoon baking powder
1 teaspoon apple cider vinegar
2 teaspoons mascarpone
60 ml heavy cream
1 teaspoon vanilla extract
1 tablespoon granulated sweetener

1. In the mixing bowl, mix coconut flour with baking powder, apple cider vinegar, mascarpone, heavy cream, vanilla extract, and sweetener. 2. Knead the dough and cut into scones. 3. Then put them half in zone 1, the remaining in zone 2, and sprinkle with cooking spray. 4. Cook the vanilla scones at 190ºC for 10 minutes.

Pumpkin Cookie with Cream Cheese Frosting

Prep time: 10 minutes | Cook time: 7 minutes | Serves 6

25 g blanched finely ground almond flour
25 g powdered sweetener, divided
2 tablespoons butter, softened
1 large egg
½ teaspoon unflavoured gelatin
½ teaspoon baking powder
½ teaspoon vanilla extract
½ teaspoon pumpkin pie spice
2 tablespoons pure pumpkin purée
½ teaspoon ground cinnamon, divided
40 g low-carb, sugar-free chocolate chips
85 g full-fat cream cheese, softened

1. In a large bowl, mix almond flour and 25 g sweetener. Stir in butter, egg, and gelatin until combined. 2. Stir in baking powder, vanilla, pumpkin pie spice, pumpkin purée, and ¼ teaspoon cinnamon, then fold in chocolate chips. 3. Pour batter into a round baking pan. Place pan into the air fryer basket. 4. Adjust the temperature to 150°C and bake for 7 minutes. 5. When fully cooked, the top will be golden brown, and a toothpick inserted in center will come out clean. Let cool at least 20 minutes. 6. To make the frosting: mix cream cheese, remaining ¼ teaspoon cinnamon, and remaining 25 g sweetener in a large bowl. Using an electric mixer, beat until it becomes fluffy. Spread onto the cooled cookie. Garnish with additional cinnamon if desired.

Eggless Farina Cake

Prep time: 30 minutes | Cook time: 25 minutes | Serves 6

Vegetable oil
470 ml hot water
165 g chopped dried fruit, such as apricots, golden raisins, figs, and/or dates
165 g very fine semolina
235 ml milk
160 g granulated sugar
55 g ghee, butter or coconut oil, melted
2 tablespoons plain Greek yogurt, or sour cream
1 teaspoon ground cardamom
1 teaspoon baking powder
½ teaspoon baking soda
Whipped cream, for serving

1. Grease a baking pan with vegetable oil. 2. In a small bowl, combine the hot water and dried fruit; set aside for 20 minutes to plump up the fruit. 3. Meanwhile, in a large bowl, whisk together the semolina, milk, sugar, ghee, yogurt and cardamom. Let stand for 20 minutes to allow the semolina to soften and absorb some of the liquid. 4. Drain the dried fruit, and gently stir it into the batter. Add the baking powder and baking soda and stir until thoroughly combined. 5. Pour the batter into the prepared pan. Set the pan in one of the air fryer baskets. Set the air fryer to 160°C, and cook for 25 minutes, or until a toothpick inserted into the center of the cake comes out clean. 6. Let the cake cool in the pan on a wire rack for 10 minutes. Remove the cake from the pan and let cool on the rack for 20 minutes before slicing. 7. Slice and serve topped with whipped cream.

Fried Cheesecake Bites

Prep time: 30 minutes | Cook time: 2 minutes | Makes 16 bites

225 g cream cheese, softened
25 g powdered sweetener, plus 2 tablespoons, divided
4 tablespoons heavy cream, divided
½ teaspoon vanilla extract
25 g almond flour

1. In a stand mixer fitted with a paddle attachment, beat the cream cheese, 50 g of the sweetener, 2 tablespoons of the heavy cream, and the vanilla until smooth. Using a small ice-cream scoop, divide the mixture into 16 balls and arrange them on a rimmed baking sheet lined with baking paper. Freeze for 45 minutes until firm. 2. Line the air fryer basket with baking paper and preheat the air fryer to 180°C. 3. In a small shallow bowl, combine the almond flour with the remaining 2 tablespoons of sweetener. 4. In another small shallow bowl, place the remaining 2 tablespoons cream. 5. One at a time, dip the frozen cheesecake balls into the cream and then roll in the almond flour mixture, pressing lightly to form an even coating. Arrange the balls in a single layer in the air fryer basket, leaving room between them. Air fry for 2 minutes until the coating is lightly browned.

Zucchini Bread

Prep time: 10 minutes | Cook time: 40 minutes | Serves 12

220 g coconut flour
2 teaspoons baking powder
150 g granulated sweetener
120 ml coconut oil, melted
1 teaspoon apple cider vinegar
1 teaspoon vanilla extract
3 eggs, beaten
1 courgette, grated
1 teaspoon ground cinnamon

1. In the mixing bowl, mix coconut flour with baking powder, sweetener, coconut oil, apple cider vinegar, vanilla extract, eggs, courgette, and ground cinnamon. 2. Transfer the mixture half in zone 1, the remaining in zone 2 and flatten it in the shape of the bread. 3. In zone 1, select Air Fry, adjust the temperature to 180°C, set the time to 40 minutes. In zone 2, select Match Cook and press Start.

Apple Fries

Prep time: 10 minutes | Cook time: 7 minutes | Serves 8

Coconut, or avocado oil, for spraying
55 g All-purpose flour
3 large eggs, beaten
100 g crushed digestive biscuits
40 g granulated sugar
1 teaspoon ground cinnamon
3 large Gala apples, peeled, cored and cut into wedges
240 ml caramel sauce, warmed

1. Preheat the air fryer to 190°C. Line the air fryer baskets with baking paper and spray lightly with oil. 2. Place the flour and beaten eggs in separate bowls and set aside. In another bowl, mix together the crushed biscuits, sugar and cinnamon. 3. Working one at a time, coat the apple wedges in the flour, dip in the egg and then dredge in the biscuit mix until evenly coated. 4. Place the apples half in zone 1, the remaining in zone 2, taking care not to overlap, and spray lightly with oil. You may need to work in batches, depending on the size of your air fryer. 5. Cook for 5 minutes, flip, spray with oil, and cook for another 2 minutes, or until crunchy and golden brown. 6. Drizzle the caramel sauce over the top and serve.

Almond Shortbread

Prep time: 10 minutes | Cook time: 12 minutes | Serves 8

110 g unsalted butter
80 g granulated sugar
1 teaspoon pure almond extract
65 g All-purpose flour

1. In bowl of a stand mixer fitted with the paddle attachment, beat the butter and sugar on medium speed until light and fluffy (3 to 4 minutes). Add the almond extract and beat until combined (about 30 seconds). Turn the mixer to low. Add the flour a little at a time and beat for about 2 minutes more until well-incorporated. 2. Pat the dough into an even layer in a baking pan. Place the pan in one of the air fryer baskets. Set the air fryer to 190°C and bake for 12 minutes. 3. Carefully remove the pan from air fryer basket. While the shortbread is still warm and soft, cut it into 8 wedges. 4. Let cool in the pan on a wire rack for 5 minutes. Remove the wedges from the pan and let cool completely on the rack before serving.

Biscuit-Base Cheesecake

Prep time: 10 minutes | Cook time: 20 minutes | Serves 8

100 g crushed digestive biscuits
3 tablespoons butter, at room temperature
225 g cream cheese, at room temperature
35 g granulated sugar
2 eggs, beaten
1 tablespoon all-purpose flour
1 teaspoon vanilla extract
60 ml chocolate syrup

1. In a small bowl, stir together the crushed biscuits and butter. Press the crust into the bottom of a 6-by-2-inch round baking pan and freeze to set while you prepare the filling. 2. In a medium bowl, stir together the cream cheese and sugar until mixed well. 3. One at a time, beat in the eggs. Add the flour and vanilla and stir to combine. 4. Transfer ⅓ of the filling to a small bowl and stir in the chocolate syrup until combined. 5. Insert the crisper plate into the basket and the basket into the unit. Preheat the air fryer to 160°C, and bake for 3 minutes. 6. Pour the vanilla filling into the pan with the crust. Drop the chocolate filling over the vanilla filling by the spoonful. With a clean butter knife stir the fillings in a zigzag pattern to marble them. Do not let the knife touch the crust. 7. Once the unit is preheated, place the pan into the basket. 8. Set the temperature to 160°C, and bake for 20 minutes. 9. When the cooking is done, the cheesecake should be just set. Cool on a wire rack for 1 hour. Refrigerate the cheesecake until firm before slicing.

Printed in Great Britain
by Amazon